BEYOND
PERSONAL
POWER

EXPERIENCING THE "GOD KIND OF FAITH"

BEYOND
PERSONAL
POWER

EXPERIENCING THE "GOD KIND OF FAITH"

BISHOP
CLARENCE E.
MCCLENDON

BEYOND PERSONAL POWER: EXPERIENCING THE "GOD KIND OF FAITH"

Clarence E. McClendon Ministries
P.O. Box 78398
Los Angeles, CA 90016
www.cemm.info

ISBN 1-880809-22-2
Printed in the United States of America
© 2003 by Clarence E. McClendon

Legacy Publishers International
1301 South Clinton Street
Denver, CO 80247
www.legacypublishersinternational.com

Cover design by: Kirk DouPonce, UDG DesignWorks
www.udgdesignworks.com

2 3 4 5 6 7 8 9 10 11 / 09 08 07 06 05 04

Table of Contents

Beyond Personal Power

Acknowledgments

First, to my Lord and Savior, Jesus Christ, who anointed me to declare His truth. I am humbled to be charged with such a responsibility, and I thank Him for His continual grace upon my life so that I may make known the power of His gospel.

To my wife, Priscilla, who continues to show me the joy of life. I thank you for sharing this work with me and encouraging me to do all that God has purposed.

To my mother, Miriam, who helped raise me in the fear of the Lord. I am blessed by your strength and your example of humility.

To the editing and research team at Siloam Bible College and Clarence E. McClendon Institute, thank you for your tireless effort to help produce the Word of God. The Lord sees your heart and will reward your obedience.

To my church family, I thank God for your maturity in releasing me to fulfill the apostolic call of God on my life.

Preface

———

The original manuscript title for this book was *Bible Faith*. Granted, "Bible Faith" does not have as much grandeur as *Beyond Personal Power*, but both describe the content accurately. The original title points out a most important concept relative to what you will learn as you read—all faith is not "Bible Faith." It isn't enough to just believe in something; you have to be able to see what you believe and *act* as if you already have it, live in it, drive it. I preached what came to be known as "Bible Faith" for almost four months to the congregation I pastor in Los Angeles; and it has literally changed the way we operate.

You'll notice some changes in yourself as you read this book. You will never look at situations the same. You definitely won't speak the same way you may speak now. As a matter of fact, you'll recognize people around you who may be church-goers and who may even have faith, but who don't have "Bible Faith." What's the difference? Well, without giving too much away (after all, I do want you to continue reading after the Preface), Bible Faith is the difference between saying "I'm broke," and *"The young lions lack and suffer hunger; but those who seek the Lord shall not lack any good thing"* (Psalm 34:10). One statement is real; the other is true.

You might say there is no difference between reality and truth; but before you read this book, you must believe the contrary. What is real is what is tangible. You can touch things that are real. The Word of God, however, is truth— *"The entirety of Your word is truth, and every one of Your righteous judgments endures forever"* (Psalm 119:160). Understanding this distinction will open your spirit to the principles you are about to learn.

To put it succinctly, if your bank account is empty, the fact that you are broke is a reality. The truth, however, is that *"those who seek the Lord shall not lack any good thing."* God has already established that you will not lack, regardless of what your bank account says. All that's left is to exercise Bible Faith until what is true becomes what is real.

We say it often in church, but as far as this book is concerned, YOUR LIFE IS ABOUT TO BE PERMANENTLY CHANGED! The sooner you begin reading, the sooner you can put these principles to work and see your situations become dictated by your obedience and the words that come out of your mouth. I am in agreement with you that everything God has promised you is done and you are being prepared to see it manifested in your life.

Be blessed and empowered,

Bishop Clarence E. McClendon

Introduction

According to the Bible, faith is the means by which righteous men and women live. However, many Christians equate believing with having faith. Contrary to traditional religious teaching, mere belief does not equal true faith. One thing that you must come to understand is that Bible Faith is very distinct from what most Christians have deduced faith to be. This has primarily resulted from a lack of being taught what Bible Faith is.

Hebrews 10:38 declares, *"Now the just shall live by faith...."* God is communicating something that is vitally important for us to understand. When He says, *"the just,"* He means those who have been made righteous by the blood of Jesus Christ (by salvation and redemption). This is a vitally important truth. God says His justified ones or those whom He has justified through the blood of Jesus, those who have been placed in right relationship with Him **shall live by this faith principle**. Faith is the means by which the righteous live.

In order to "live by faith," you must know what "God says faith is" is and how to obtain it. Contrary to popular religious teaching, mere belief in the Lord's promises is not true faith unless accompanied by a corresponding action. To truly walk by faith, a believer must keep hearing the Word of God to remain convinced of any preordained promise. James chapter 2 teaches us that **faith equals conviction** or **persuasion plus corresponding action**.

> *What does it profit, my brethren, if someone says he has faith* [conviction or persuasion] *but does not have* [corresponding] *works? Can faith save him?...Thus also faith by itself, if it does not have works, is dead. But someone will say, "You have faith, and I have works." Show me your faith without your works, and I will show you my faith by my works. You believe that there is one God. You do well. Even the demons believe—and tremble!* (James 2:14,17-19)

By applying the principles outlined in this book, you will learn how to live by the "God-Kind of Faith" and come to the realization that true faith is what prompts us to carry out acts in the natural realm that bring God's promises to pass. As you begin to get this powerful truth on the inside and begin speaking what you believe in accordance with the Word of God, I want you to write me and tell me all that God is doing in your life. I pray the Holy Spirit opens the eyes of your understanding and grants you revelation as you read. I pray you may

Introduction

know His power, and experience the tangible presence of God on your life as you put true Bible Faith truth into effect and begin living life *Beyond Personal Power*.

Beyond Personal Power

Have Bible Faith

Chapter 1

Have Bible Faith

M any Christians today equate belief with faith. However, contrary to traditional religious teaching, believing alone is not true faith. The Bible provides a working blueprint of the kind of faith that will move you into God's purpose for your life. God wants you to fully receive all the promises of His Word. Therefore, you must know whether or not you are walking in true faith.

Recently, the Spirit of God has taken me through a faith examination. In Second Corinthians 13:5, the apostle Paul writes, *"Examine yourselves as to whether you are in **the** faith..."* (emphasis added). The word *the* does not appear in the original, but was added during translation for clarification. The original (Greek) text actually reads: "Examine yourselves as to whether you are in faith." *To examine* means to "observe carefully or critically," or "to check the condition of." So, Paul is saying to critically and carefully observe yourself—check to see what kind of condition you are in relative to faith and pay attention to see whether or not you are in faith. *Examine* also means "to determine the qualifications of." In other words, *find out what qualifies you to be in faith* and make sure you measure up to it. The reality of your situation is not what I say it is, and it is not what you say it is; it is what God's Word says it is.

I want to begin with a foundational definition of Bible Faith. By "Bible Faith," I am referring to what God means when He says "faith." This is important because the Word of God says that *"without faith it is impossible to please Him"* (Hebrews 11:6), and *"the just shall live by faith"* (Hebrews 10:38). If without faith it is impossible to please God, and if the just (or those who have been justified or made right with God) shall live by faith, then it is not something we can afford to be confused about as justified men or women made right with God by the blood of Jesus.

According to Scripture, *"the just shall live by faith."* Therefore, they shall not live by church attendance, church membership, or by being under the ministry of a preacher they like. The just shall live by faith. It is not faith according to my definition or your definition of faith, but faith according to the definition of God's Word. This is important because He is the one who is supplying what you need. He is the one who has promised to heal your body.

Just like the commercial in which the kid asks, "Is it soup yet?" you must ask yourself, "Is it faith yet?" It is not soup until all the ingredients are there to make it soup. You and I must ask if all the ingredients are there to make it faith. I am talking about Bible Faith. You might say, "Bishop, you are straining at a gnat here—this is a small thing"; but it is **not** a small thing. Let me give you an example of how important it is to have the right definition.

A few years ago, there was a word introduced into the youth culture by the hip-hop community—*phat*. Left and right, you could hear kids saying, "That's phat," or "That's a phat ride," or "Man, you're looking phat." If someone would say to you, "You are looking phat," and you just finished a 90-day stint at *Jenny Craig* or *Weight Watchers*, you would be insulted. You must understand what the word *phat* means to the person using it, in order to understand that he is not saying you are overweight. If you do not understand what *phat* means in that culture, and are working off the traditional definition of *"fat,"* you will not understand that "You look phat" is actually a compliment. In other words, if you tell a person who does not have the same definition of "phat" as you do that they look "phat," you could get a very negative reaction, and then you will wonder why you did not get the response you expected.

Religion has given us a definition of faith, which if we have not been taught otherwise or studied the Word of God for ourselves, most of us accept. Most of us have accepted it because it is what we have been taught by our mother, father, or preacher, but we really do not know what God means when He says "faith." The general consensus of most Christians is that faith means belief. When we believe something, we say, "I have faith." What I want

4

you to understand is that, according to God's Word, believing is not faith. **Something must be added to believing to make it Bible Faith.**

That is the way most Christians are when it comes to faith. We offer up to God what we think and have been taught is faith, but do not get the response we expect because our def- *"Believing is not* inition of faith is not the same as His. It is not Bible Faith. So, the Spirit of *faith. And faith* the Lord said to me earnestly, "Son, I want you to examine yourself." As I *is not merely* began to do so, I saw some areas where I was absolutely in faith and *believing."* other areas where I had let my faith slip or had missed the mark due to a faulty definition of what faith is.

It is important that we understand God's definition of faith because although God is not a legalist, Satan is. God is not sitting in Heaven checking things off a list, "Check, check, check, okay, I can give it to you," but the devil is. God is righteous and He will not allow the adversary to accuse Him or call Him a liar. Because God's Word says, *"The just shall live by faith,"* God has restrained Himself by His Word from acting on behalf of the just unless the just **live** this way: by faith as His Word defines it. If the just do not meet the criteria or standard set forth in God's Word, but He still gives them what they are believing for, the adversary can accuse God of lying—and God will not allow that. His Word says, *"God is not a man, that He should lie"* (Numbers 23:19). So, we must learn what Bible Faith is (what God says faith is), and walk by that standard. When you do, you will beat the devil in every area of your life.

Beyond Personal Power

Jesus said in Luke 10:19, *"I give unto you power to **tread** on serpents and scorpions, and over all the power of the enemy; and nothing shall by any means hurt you"* (KJV, emphasis added). The Bible also says that, *"We **walk** by faith, not by sight"* (2 Corinthians 5:7, emphasis added). To tread is to walk, so if Jesus says, "I give you power to tread," what He is telling you is that the power to tread is the walk of faith. Bible Faith gives you power. When you learn to walk by Bible Faith—not religious faith—*then* you will tread on serpents and scorpions.

"Bible Faith releases divine power in your situation."

To find out what God means when He says "faith," we must go to the second chapter in the Book of James.

> *What does it profit, my brethren, if someone says he has **faith** but does not have **works**? Can faith save him? If a brother or sister is naked and destitute of daily food, and one of you says to them, "Depart in peace, be warmed and filled," but you do not give them the things which are needed for the body, what does it profit? Thus also, faith by itself, if it does not have works, is dead* (James 2:14-17, emphasis added).

In James, the word *faith* is the Greek word *pistis*, which means "conviction or persuasion." In other words, *pistis* means to be convicted or persuaded about something. The word *works* in James chapter 2, is the Greek word *ergon*. This is the word from which we get the English word *energy*. The Greek word *ergon* means "corresponding action." A corresponding action is an action that responds to your conviction, your persuasion, or what you say you believe. And so, if we insert these terms—"conviction" or "persuasion" and "corresponding action"—where we see the words *faith* and *works* in James 2, we have the beginning of our working definition of faith. For example, replacing *faith* and *works* with our working definition as we continue in James chapter 2 reads:

> *What does it profit, my brethren, if some- one says he has* [conviction or persua- sion] *but does not have* [corresponding action]? *Can* [conviction or persua- sion] *save him? If a brother or sister is naked and destitute of daily food, and one of you says to them, "Depart in peace, be warmed and filled," but you do not give them the things which are need- ed for the body, what does it profit? Thus also* [conviction or persuasion] *by itself, if it does not have* [correspon- ding action] *is dead* (James 2:14-17).

"Greek Translations: Pistis: to be convicted or persuaded. Ergon: corresponding action."

James 2:14-17 tells us that faith can be living or dead. Because if there is such a thing as "dead faith," there has to be such a thing as "living faith." Faith can be dead because it has no works—no corresponding action. **Living faith** is conviction or persuasion *plus* corresponding action. This distinction between living and dead faith is very important. Every place the Bible refers to faith in the New Covenant, God is talking about *living* faith. The Bible is never talking about dead faith when it is talking about faith.

Beyond Personal Power

I understand that most people have been taught, and therefore believe, that faith is defined in Hebrews 11:1:

"Divine Principle:

Living faith =

conviction or

persuasion +

corresponding

action =

Bible Faith."

"Now faith is the substance of things hoped for, the evidence of things not seen." I do not wish to argue with that. Some people teach it that way and it works for them, but it does not work for me. I need a definition that I can put anywhere I see the word *faith* and get a clearer understanding of what faith is. I believe that Hebrews 11:1 provides the anatomy of faith; it tells us the substance of which faith is made. But when I read, *"Daughter, thy faith has made thee whole,"* I cannot replace the word *faith* with that definition and get an understanding of faith—*"Daughter,* [the substance of things hoped for and the evidence of things not seen] *has made thee whole."* That definition of faith does not tell me what faith is; it does not tell me what made the daughter whole. James chapter 2 gives me a working definition. If we insert the words *conviction or persuasion* everywhere we read the word *faith*, and insert the words *corresponding action* everywhere we read the word *works*, and clearly understand what it means, then the definition of *faith* comes alive.

The majority of Christians, when they speak of faith, are saying, "I believe." What they mean is they believe something, or are convinced or persuaded about it, but they never add the corresponding action to their conviction or persuasion that causes it to become Bible Faith.

Understand this, child of God: When God says, *"The just shall live by faith,"* He is telling you the just shall live by this kind of faith—**conviction or persuasion plus corresponding action**. God is saying, "Everywhere I call upon you to have faith, or everywhere I call upon you to walk by faith, I am calling upon you to walk by living faith because that is the only definition of faith that My Word gives you. My Word does not acknowledge or accept the other kind as faith. I know that your church told you it was, but My Word did not tell you it was."

Continuing in James 2, beginning with verse 18 and replacing the words *faith* and *works* with our working definition gives us an even clearer understanding of what God means when He says faith.

> *But someone will say, "You have* [conviction or persuasion] *and I have* [corresponding actions]*." Show me your* [conviction or persuasion] *without your* [corresponding actions]*, and I will show you my* [conviction or persuasion] *by my* [corresponding action]*. You believe that there is one God. You do well. Even the demons believe—and tremble! But do you want to know, O foolish man, that* [conviction or persuasion] *without* [corresponding actions] *is dead? Was not Abraham our father justified by* [corresponding actions]*…?* (James 2:18-21)

The Bible says Abraham was justified—or made right with God—not just by what he believed, but rather when his actions corresponded to what he believed. *"Was not Abraham our father justified by works when he offered Isaac his son on the altar?"* (James 2:21) When Abraham offered Isaac on the altar, his conviction or persuasion and corresponding action worked together. *"Do you see that faith* [conviction or persuasion] *was **working together** with his works* [corresponding action], *and by works* [corresponding action] *faith* (conviction or persuasion) *was made perfect?"* (James 2:22, emphasis added) The word *perfect* means "mature, complete or finished." Because of his corresponding action, his conviction or persuasion was made perfect. In other words, Abraham's corresponding action worked together with his belief [conviction or persuasion] to make his faith complete. *"And the Scripture was fulfilled which says, 'Abraham believed God, and it was accounted to him for righteousness' "* (James 2:23). In other words, the Scripture was fulfilled when Abraham's conviction or persuasion met up with his corresponding action.

This is what the Bible means when it instructs us to "believe." How many of you want God to finish the promise He made you? For those of you who do, the formula is to get your conviction or persuasion working together with your corresponding action.

Because the Scripture that says *"Abraham believed God"* (James 2:23) was not fulfilled until Abraham's conviction or persuasion met up with his corresponding action, I know it is not enough to simply be convicted or persuaded. This tells me that there must be a corresponding action with my conviction. Therefore, to say, "I believe God," is not enough. My belief alone is not living faith.

Continuing on and beginning at James 2:24, again we replace "faith" and "works" with our working definition: *"You see then that a man is justified* [or made right with God] *by* [corresponding actions], *and not by* [conviction or

10

persuasion] *only. Likewise, was not Rahab the harlot also justified by* [corresponding actions] *when she received the messengers and sent them out another way?"* (James 2:24-25) There was action when she **received** and **sent**. The Bible says, *"He sent His word and healed them"* (Psalm 107:20). This tells me that Bible Faith is when you receive and send the Word of God.

Another example that shows the necessity of having conviction or persuasion plus corresponding action is seen in James 2:26: *"For as the body without the spirit is dead, so faith without works is dead also."* These ingredients are required for life in

"Your corresponding actions give life to your conviction or persuasion."

human beings: body plus spirit. If the spirit leaves the body, the individual no longer exists. It is the spirit that gives life to the body. So, the Bible states that just like it takes the spirit to give life to the body, it also takes corresponding action to give life to your conviction or persuasion. The corresponding action is the life-giving part, not the belief. It is the corresponding action that gives life to your conviction or persuasion. Both together make your faith complete.

Second Corinthians 4:13-14 reads, *"And since we have the same spirit of faith, according to what is written, 'I believed and therefore I spoke,' we also believe and therefore speak, knowing that He who raised up the Lord Jesus will also raise us up with Jesus, and will present us with you."* This word *spirit* is the Greek word *pneuma,* which means vital principle and mental disposition. So, when Paul says, *"We have the same spirit of faith,"* he is saying we have the mental disposition of faith. In Psalm 116:10, when David says, *"I believed, therefore*

I spoke," he is referring to this same vital principle and mental disposition of faith. Continuing in Psalm 116, David says, *"I believed, therefore I spoke, 'I am greatly afflicted.' "* **He believed he was greatly afflicted and spoke that he was greatly afflicted. Therefore, he stayed greatly afflicted.** I will discuss this in greater detail later, but faith works both ways. Whatever you believe, you will speak, and whatever you speak, you will have because you were created in the image and the likeness of God. God is a Spirit who speaks what He believes and it comes to pass, and so are you.

"The Vital Principle of Faith: Faith speaks what it believes."

That is why the key to walking by faith is making sure you believe the right thing, for if you believe the right thing, you will speak the right thing. And if you speak the right thing, you will have the right thing.

Another way to think of it is an *attitude* of faith. To walk by faith, you must have a faith attitude. The vital principle or attitude of faith is that **faith speaks what it believes**. Speaking what you believe is the first corresponding action of your faith. Faith also has a mental disposition. What is the mental disposition of faith? Faith is always **is**. When speaking what you believe, always speak in the present tense. Faith is never *going to* happen. Faith is never "God will make a way" or "God is going to heal me." You may believe it, but that does not make it faith; and if it is not faith, God is not obligated to move on it. He will not respond to "going to." He is not the "Great I am going to," He is the "Great I AM," and faith *is* always present tense. *"The word is near* *you in your mouth and in your heart"* (Romans 10:8). Not the words *will be,* but the word *is.* Faith says, "the word *is*" and the promise of God *is* now, not "will be." Faith does not say, "I am going to be healed." Faith says, "by His stripes, I am healed." Faith does not say, "I am going to be prospered," but faith declares that "I am prospered now" because it is a done deal. God is not going to do anything. Everything that God is going

"Mental Disposition of Faith: Faith is always present tense."

to do is already done. If He has done it, then it is finished or complete, and faith is always "**is.**"

> *Now the next day, when they had come out from Bethany, He was hungry. And seeing from afar a fig tree having leaves, He went to see if perhaps He would find something on it. When He came to it, He found nothing but leaves, for it was not the season for figs. In response Jesus said to it, "Let no one eat fruit from you ever again." And His disciples heard it….Now in the morning, as they passed by, they saw the fig tree dried up from the roots. And Peter, remembering, said to Him, "Rabbi, look! The fig tree which You cursed has withered away." So Jesus answered and said to them, "Have faith in God* [literally: the God kind of faith]. *For assuredly, I say to you, whoever says to this mountain, 'Be removed and be cast into the sea,' and does not doubt in his heart, but believes that those things he says will be done, he will have whatever he says. Therefore, I say to you, whatever things you ask when you pray, believe that you receive them, and you will have them"* (Mark 11:12-14,20-24).

Beyond Personal Power

Here Jesus tells His disciples to "have the God-Kind of Faith" because His dealing with this fig tree has just exemplified what the God-Kind of Faith is. The God-Kind of Faith speaks what it believes, or what it wants to happen, based on the Word of God. It speaks God's Word in the present tense in response to those situations and circumstances in life that come against it. *Now, if you are not speaking what you believe in the present tense, first of all, it is not Bible Faith.* The God-Kind of Faith is a brand of faith to which only the believer has access. Remember, the vital principle and the mental disposition of faith from Second Corinthians 4 is that faith speaks what it believes. The mental disposition or mind-set of faith from Romans 10 is that the Word *is*, or that what the Word says *is* happening now.

I had problems with this concept for years. Because of the way people taught it, I did not fully understand it. So, I asked God to give me revelation. He said, "Speaking is the vital principle of faith." Understand that it is not your confession that makes anything happen because anything that you are confessing based on God's Word is already done. But, in order for you to see things manifest in your life, you must *walk by the vital principle of faith.* Remember, faith is **conviction** or **persuasion** plus **corresponding action**. So, when the Bible refers to the *spirit* (of faith) or *vital principle* (mental disposition) of faith, God is telling you that the vital principle of acting on what you believe is speaking what you believe. God is telling you that you will not act on what you believe until you begin speaking what you believe. This is because you were created to do what you speak.

Now, put this all together: Because faith is conviction or persuasion plus corresponding action and the vital principle of being a person walking in faith is speaking what you believe, then you will not act on what you believe unless you discipline yourself to speak what you believe. Think about it. Right now, you are acting on what you have spoken in the past. The problem is, most of us speak whatever comes into our minds—whatever experience tells us. Because you are speaking what your experience has told you, you are continuing to experience the same thing. Remember, you were created in the image of God. What you speak comes to pass in your life. Just because humanity fell into sin does not mean that God changed the function of His creation. His creation still sees or experiences what it speaks. The problem is, that, in sin, His creation lost the ability to see what it was supposed to see or experience. That is why He wrote you a letter—the living Word, the Bible—to tell you what you lost and give you ability to see, so you could then speak it by His Word.

"The God-Kind of Faith speaks what it wants to happen based on the Word in the present tense."

Continuing on, the word *vital* means necessary for the continuation of life. A vital sign is a signal that indicates life. When you go to the hospital, they check your vital signs as an indicator upon which the doctor determines whether or not you are alive. If you have vital signs, you have life in you. If you do not have vital signs, there is no indication of life and the conclusion is that you are dead. When God tells us that speaking what we believe is the vital principle of faith, He is saying **that the action of our speaking is the principle upon which He determines whether or not we are walking by faith. It is the vital one, the necessary one.** In the past, I struggled with the whole confession principle until God set it in my spirit that I was created in the image of a God who speaks things into existence. I was created to see what I speak. If it is not being spoken, it is not faith yet. *Belief stays quiet, but faith speaks.* Belief alone is not going to accomplish anything. Bible Faith—conviction or persuasion plus corresponding action—is the victory that overcomes the world, not our believing. In order for your faith to live, the vital principle of faith is that faith speaks what it believes. And faith always speaks what it believes in the present tense.

"If it is not being spoken, it is not faith yet."

> *...I believed and therefore I spoke, we also believe and therefore speak, knowing that He who raised up the Lord Jesus will also raise us up with Jesus, and will present us with you* (2 Corinthians 4:13-14).

Now please, do not miss this principle. Now that we know the vital principle and the mental disposition of faith, that faith speaks what it believes in the present tense' Paul said we speak what we believe knowing that what God did for Jesus, He will do for us. The God who raised Jesus up from the dead also will raise us up. What was he saying? We know that what God did for Jesus, He will do for us.

16

Everything God does, He does by faith. Jesus was resurrected because He did what I am teaching you. The power that was available for Jesus' resurrection was made available because Jesus exercised these principles. God, the Father, raised Jesus up using these principles. We can see this in John 10:17-18. Jesus is speaking and He says, *"Therefore My Father loves Me, because I lay down My life that I may take it again. No one takes it from Me, but I lay it down of Myself. I have power to lay it down, and I have power to take it again. This command I have received from My Father."* Here Jesus is saying, "No man takes My life; I lay it down. I have the **power** to lay it down, and I have the power to take it up again. **This command I have received from My Father.**" In other words, Jesus is saying that because His Father said this to Him, it is the Father's Word, not Jesus' word. The Father told Him He had the power to lay it down and the power to pick it up again. *He is saying it because the Father said it to Him. Jesus is speaking His Father's Word concerning His own life.* Understand that *no one* had ever done what Jesus was about to do. At the moment when Jesus says, *"I have the power to lay it down, and I have the power to take it up again,"* He does not actually **have** that power in manifestation. At that moment, He says, "I have the power," but He does not possess it at that moment, because He does not need the power at that moment.

Jesus knows that God will supply all His need. Although He does not need the power to lay down His life at that moment, He knows He is going to need the power in the future. *Therefore, He says He has the power now*. When He gets to the situation where He needs the power, it will then be too late to say, "I have the power." He says He has it *before* He needs it, so it will be there when He does need it.

In the Garden of Gethsemane, Jesus is struggling in His humanity to lay down His life. As He struggles in His humanity, He prays, "*O My Father, if it is possible, let this cup pass from Me...*" (Matthew 26:39). In other words, if there is any other way to accomplish what needs to be done, then I would like to do it that way. In that instance, Jesus does not sound to me like someone who has the power to lay His life down. He is struggling with laying it down. He is fighting to keep Himself from going the route that the Father has commanded. But, remember, before He got there, He had put into effect the vital principle of faith (faith speaks what it believes). Before Jesus arrived at the moment when He needed the power to lay down His life, He spoke, "*I have power to lay it down, and I have power to take it again*" (John 10:18). Because He had spoken it, when He got to the place where He was struggling, His confession of faith met Him in the garden and the power of God was released on His behalf. This is how Bible Faith works: It speaks what it believes.

Know What Bible Faith Is

Chapter 2

Know What Bible Faith Is

———◆◆◆———

We have laid the foundation of the vital principle and mental disposition of Bible Faith. In this chapter, I reveal the elements that determine what it means to have the God-Kind of Faith. Mark 11:12-14, our foundational text for this chapter, gives us an example of what it means to have the God-Kind of Faith:

> *Now the next day, when they had come out from Bethany, He was hungry. And seeing from afar a fig tree having leaves, He went to see if perhaps He would find something on it. When He came to it, He found nothing but leaves, for it was not the season for figs.* **In response** *Jesus said to it, "Let no one eat fruit from you ever again." And His disciples heard it* (emphasis added).

Notice, the Bible says *"in response."* In order for the Bible to say "in response," the fig tree must have been *saying something* to Jesus that He had to respond to. You might ask how an inanimate object spoke to Him. We see here that this is what the fight of faith is. Just like the fig tree was saying something to Jesus, your situation is speaking to you all the time. It is telling you that you do not have enough. Your lack is talking to you. Your pain is talking to you. The problem is, you are not answering back. *Holler back* to it! You have to stop letting your circumstance talk to you and you not *holler back*. The man or woman of faith does not allow a circumstance to talk to them—to work on their mind—without speaking back. Jesus saw a barren fig tree and the Bible says, "He said **in response**," which meant that He was communicating back to His circumstance of barrenness and lack, which was talking to Him. If you are going to live and walk in the God-Kind of Faith, you have to *holler back*! You cannot allow lack, sickness, and disease to talk to you and not say something back. You cannot allow negative circumstances to speak and work on your mind and not speak back. But you have to discipline your holler to make sure that the Word of God is coming out of your mouth.

"Your situation is speaking to you. You must respond to it with the Word of God. You must holler back."

In the King James Bible, the Scripture shows us another element of the God-Kind of Faith. Jesus says in Mark 11:14, *"No man eat fruit of thee **hereafter** for ever"* (emphasis added). The translation here is "Let no one eat fruit of you now or later." As we have previously learned, faith is always present tense. Let no one eat fruit of you *here* or *after*. This statement covers two dimensions of time *and* is in present tense. Verse 14 reads, "*And Jesus answered and said unto it, No man eat fruit of thee hereafter for ever. And His disciples heard it.*" Faith speaks loud enough for someone else to hear it. Faith does not only mumble to itself, but faith speaks to be heard, and it really does not matter who else hears, as long as you talk loud enough for you and God to hear you. In verse 14, His disciples heard it.

"*Divine Principle: Faith speaks loud enough for others to hear.*"

> *Now in the morning, as they passed by, they saw the fig tree dried up from the roots. And Peter, remembering, said to Him, "Rabbi, look! The fig tree which You cursed has withered away." So Jesus answered and said to them, "**Have faith in God**"* (Mark 11:20-22, emphasis added).

In the original Greek, it is translated, "Have the God-Kind of Faith."

> *For assuredly, I say to you, whoever says to this mountain, "Be removed and be cast into the sea," and does not doubt in his heart, but believes that those things he says will be done, he will have whatever he says. Therefore I say to you, whatever things you ask when you pray, **believe that you receive them**, and you will have them* (Mark 11:23-24, emphasis added).

Get this: The Bible says in Mark 11:24, "*Therefore I say to you, whatever things you ask when you pray, believe that you receive them, and you will have them.*" It says "**when you pray.**"

Not when you **see**, but believe you receive when you **pray**. You may be wondering why this is. If I pray and I believe I receive, then the moment after I pray, I say, "I have." Remember, Bible Faith is conviction or persuasion plus corresponding action. When you declare that you have what you just prayed for, that is a form of corresponding action. He says when you pray, believe you receive, because if you believe you receive when you pray, right after you pray, you say "I have." And if

"When we pray, we must believe we receive. The moment after we pray, we say, 'I have.'"

you say, "I have," then what you say will come to pass.

I want you to pay attention to this. Jesus, after exemplifying this to His disciples, tells them to have "the God-Kind of Faith." Within a 24-hour period after Jesus spoke to this fig tree, it was dried up from the roots. They were coming in one day from Bethany to Jerusalem. He saw the fig tree, spoke to it, they did their ministry for a day in Jerusalem, and went back to Bethany. It was night then, so they could not see the fig tree. Then the next morning, as they got back up and were going back into Jerusalem, Peter said, *"Master! The fig tree you cursed has withered away."* Within 24 hours! See, the God-Kind of Faith can change a situation within 24 hours!

Faith is a law of God. In the Book of Romans, the Bible talks about the law of faith. Just like gravity is a law, faith is a law that works for the sinner or saint alike. I will give you an example. If I, as a believer, jump off a 20-story building and an unbeliever right next to me jumps off the same 20-story building at the same time, which one of us will go splat? Both of us will. Whether I am a believer or an unbeliever, the law of gravity is going to work because it is a divine law in the earth. Faith is the same way. It works for the believer or the unbeliever. It is a law, but the believer has the opportunity and the privilege to have the God-Kind of Faith.

Now this means that faith has quality—it has levels. Let me put it to you like this: There are different "brands" of faith. For example, when I was in college, I had a Dodge Omni. It was a little, white, tennis shoe-looking car. It was an automobile—it had four wheels, a steering wheel, seats, and a gas tank. If you filled it up, it would go putt, putt, putt wherever you directed it. It was a brand of car. Today I drive a Bentley—Rolls Royce family. It was given to me as a gift.

"Faith is a divine law—like the law of gravity—that works for the believer or unbeliever alike. But the believer has the opportunity to have the God-Kind of Faith."

What I want you to understand here is that the Omni and the Bentley are both automobiles, but they are different brands of automobiles. They are different levels of the same thing called a car. The Omni will get you where you want to go. The Bentley, however, gets you where you want to go in another atmosphere. The Omni has a plastic environment. The Bentley has a handcrafted leather and polished barrel-wood environment. The Omni will get you where you want to go. However, a Bentley (with its twin-turbo, V8 engine) will get you there much faster. I want to emphasize an important point here. I am showing you two different levels of the same thing. The Bentley will get you where you need to go faster than the Omni, and that is what the God-Kind of Faith will do.

The God-Kind of Faith escalates how you get where you are going. It changes the ride, alters the atmosphere of your journey, and causes you to arrive in an entirely different style. You do not look all rumpled, torn up, and broken down when you finally arrive. I am talking about the God-Kind of Faith.

We know that faith speaks what it believes in the present tense, and that is a principle of faith. What you must understand is that you are living by faith, right now, because you are getting what you believe. The problem is you may be believing the wrong set of things. Therefore, you are speaking the wrong set of things because your believing is based on the wrong set of realities. When your bank account says zero, you are saying that you are not going to be able to pay your bills because your experience (or the experience of the people around you) has demonstrated to you that when the checkbook says "zero," bills are not paid. That has been your experience, and because that is what you have seen, that is what you believe. And because that is what you believe, that is what you speak. Remember, faith speaks what it believes and gets what it says. You have been speaking, "I do not have enough money," and you have not had enough money.

Now Jesus says, "I want you to learn how to live on another level. I want you to discipline yourselves to have the God-Kind of Faith." The God-Kind of Faith is the kind of faith that speaks what it believes based on God's Word in the present tense. Mark 11:23 reads, *"For assuredly, I say to you, whoever says to this mountain, 'Be removed and be cast into the sea….' "* What is He saying here? He is not telling us to speak to everything and tell it to go into the sea. If you tell your debt to be removed and cast into the sea, all you end up with is wet debt. What Jesus is teaching us here is that the God-Kind of Faith speaks what it wants to happen. I say to the mountain, "Be removed and be cast into the sea," because that is what I want to happen to the mountain. That is not what I want to happen with my debt. I do not want my debt to go into the sea. I want my debt to go where it belongs— into my past.

Jesus is teaching a powerful principle here. He says, "If you say to the mountain." The key word here is *"say."* You must speak what you want to happen based on God's Word. You may be wondering, *Where do you get the "based on God's Word"?* Look at Mark 11:23: "*…and does not doubt in his heart, but believes that those things he says will be done, he will have whatever he says.*" Jesus is saying, "If you can get to the place where you believe what you say will be done, you will have what you say." Get this: **If you can get to the place that you believe what you say will be done, you will have what you say**. This means my challenge is getting to the place and staying in the place where I believe what I say will be done.

I struggled with this for years until I was meditating upon the Word, and the Spirit of God spoke to me. He said, "Son, do you know how to make sure you believe what you say will come to pass?" I said, "How?" He said, "Just say what I said." Do you believe what God says? If not, it is probably because you have broken your own word to you. You have broken your own word to you so many times that you do not even believe what you say will come to pass. But do you believe that what God says will come to pass? Jesus said, *"Heaven and earth will pass away before one jot or tittle* [literally, before one comma or period] *of my word passes away."*

The challenge is getting myself to believe the things that I say will come to pass. The Lord said to me, "It is very easy; just stop saying what you want to say and start saying what I said, because you already believe that what I said will come to pass. The problem is you have not been saying what I said; you have been saying what you want to say. Every time a situation comes up to you, you respond to it with what you want to say instead of what I said." He said, "If you will train yourself, discipline yourself, correct yourself, and get yourself to where My Word is what is coming out of your mouth, you will not have any problem believing that what you say will come to pass." The challenge is making sure you believe that what you say will come to pass.

"Your head has nothing to do with your faith. Romans 10:10 says, 'With the heart man believes.' God says, 'If you speak My Word, your heart believes it.'"

Let me state another important truth to you about the God-Kind of Faith. Again, Mark 11:23 says, *"…and does not doubt in his heart, but believes…."* It does not say anything about the head. See, your head is not the key to your faith. Romans 10:10 says, *"With the heart one believes."* It does not say, "With the heart one has to try to believe." It says, *"With the heart one believes."* See, you do believe with your heart. The Word says you do; the problem is that we have not defined believing by the Word but by our experience. God says if you speak this Word, your heart

27

believes it. In essence if you are confessing, you are believing with your heart. "**Confess**" in Greek is the word *homologeo: homo* meaning "same," and *logos* meaning "word." To confess is to say the same word. When you are saying the same thing God says, He calls that believing with your heart.

Regardless of what your head is telling you, **if you say what God said, you are believing with your heart**. He is the one who has set this up, so His rules apply. Listen, you can be terrified and feeling like you are going to lose your mind, but God says, "If you are saying what I am saying, you are believing with your heart and you will have whatever you say." God is saying that if you are saying with your mouth what His Word has said and you are believing with your heart, then it does not matter what is going on in your head. You will have what you say.

David discovered this and learned this vital lesson in Psalm 116:10-11. He says, *"I believed, therefore I spoke, 'I am greatly afflicted.' I said in my haste, 'All men are liars.' "* And this is where I discovered David is telling us the vital principle and the mental disposition of faith. "I believed I was greatly afflicted, I said I was greatly afflicted, and so I stayed greatly afflicted. I said *'in my haste, All men are liars,'* and guess what happened? I was surrounded by a bunch of liars, cutthroats, thieves, and my own son, Absalom, tried to betray me and take the kingdom from me because I was saying, 'all men are liars.' " And he said, "I said it in my haste." I said it without thinking; I said it without stopping. I said it without disciplining myself. I said it without watching what came out of my mouth, so I did what was I called a time-out. Take a *time-*

out. Think before you respond negatively to your circumstance. David did.

He goes on to say in verse 12, *"What shall I render to the Lord?"* See, we use this Scripture for offering. David was not talking about money here. He was saying, "What shall I say, what should be coming out of my mouth to God, what shall I render?" And then he says, *"I will take up the cup of salvation."* Now, what do you do from a cup? You drink from it, and what happens to what you drink? It gets inside you! Get the Word of God in you, and make sure it is the Word of God coming out of your mouth in response to your situation. Take and drink from the cup. *"Whoever drinks of the water that I shall give him will never thirst"* (John 4:14). God is saying, if you get this in you—My Word in your heart, for out of the abundance of the heart the mouth speaks—you will get what you say and you will never thirst again!

Beyond Personal Power

Chapter 3

Speak What You Believe

Chapter 3

Speak What You Believe

———❖———

Remember that according to James chapter 2, Bible Faith is "conviction or persuasion plus corresponding action." Faith also has a vital principle and a mental disposition. In Second Corinthians 4:13, the apostle writes, *"We have the same spirit of faith, according to what is written, 'I believed and therefore I spoke.' "* The word *spirit* here is not referring to an entity or deity, but rather means *vital principle and/or mental disposition.* So, when Paul says, "We have the spirit of faith," he is saying, **we have the vital principle and mental disposition of faith**. Remember, *vital* means *"foundational, necessary for life."* There are other corresponding actions to faith, but this is the first and the foremost corresponding action to your faith. **The vital principle of faith is that "faith speaks what it believes."** Faith also has a mental disposition or mind-set.

There is a way that a person who is walking or living by faith has his or her mind-set. The mind-set of faith is **that faith is always present tense**.

When Jesus says in John 10:10, *"I have come that they may have life, and that they may have it more abundantly,"* He uses the word *zoe*. The Greek word *zoe* means life. So, in order to experience the God-Kind of life, you have got to exercise the God-Kind of Faith.

In His earthly ministry, Jesus was, and still is, "the Living Word." Therefore, everything that came out of His mouth was "the living Word of God." When you look at the ministry of Jesus, you have to understand that, or else you will not be able to distinguish between how He could speak to situations and see results, and when you speak to them and nothing changes. The difference is that everything He spoke was "the living Word," and therefore, everything He said affected the circumstance. So, He could speak "peace" to the wind and say, "be still" to a wave and there would be a great calm because He had just spoken "the living Word." He could say to a sick man, "Your sins are forgiven" and it would be so because He had just spoken "the living Word."

In order to get those same results, we have to make sure that what is coming out of our mouths is "the living Word." I am not "the living Word," and neither are you—I know you are special, but you are not there yet—you are *not* "the living Word." To get the God-Kind of results, we have to make sure that we do what Jesus did, and that is to speak the Word of God to your circumstance and situation. You must holler back. Jesus did not have to think about it because that was all that was in Him. He did not have to go to the Scripture, get promises and renew His mind to it because His mind did not need renewing. His mind had never tasted of sin and did not have to recover from a fallen state. It did not have to come back from negative experience. Our minds do, and that is why we must renew our minds to the Word of God and make sure that the Word of God is coming out of our mouths.

Since everything that came out of Him was the Word, He could respond immediately to everything. He could spiritually respond immediately. He could respond without stopping. He could respond without taking a time-out. Everything in Him was the living Word, but it is not so with you and I. We have our experiences, our lower nature to contend with. We have things that are still in us. What we have to do before we *holler back* to our situations is make sure that what is in our mouths is the living Word. We have to say, "Wait, I am not going to respond out of my emotion; I am not going to say what I feel." Do you see this?

God Himself exercises this very principle in order to affect change and bring the desired results that He wanted in the earth. This is how Jesus lived, worked miracles, and walked in power. Although Jesus was "the Living Word" in His earthly ministry, He also was in the flesh. He was 100 percent man and 100 percent God. The Jesus part of Him was 100 percent man; and the Christ part of Him, which was on the inside, was 100 percent God. So everything He did, He accomplished as a man anointed with the Spirit of God within Him. It is important to understand this because, if you do not, you will look at His ministry, words, and accomplishments, and say, "Well, He did that because He was Jesus." No, He did it because He disciplined Himself to not allow anything to come out of His mouth that was not God's living Word. If you do what Jesus did, you will have the Jesus-Kind of results because that is the God-Kind of Faith.

Many people think that because Jesus was the Son of God, He knew everything from birth—He knew who He was, what He was going to do, and the complete and total will of God. Not so. He had to learn the plan and will of God just like you and I do because in His earthly ministry, He ministered as *a man* anointed with the Holy Ghost. Look at Luke 2:40: "*And the Child grew and became strong in spirit, filled with wisdom; and the grace of God was upon Him.*" Concerning Jesus of Nazareth, the Bible says that "*the Child grew and became strong in spirit.*" Now, if He *became* strong in spirit as He was growing, that means He did not start off as strong in spirit as He was later. You do not become something if you are already it. To become something means going from one state to another state. Saying that "you became rich" means you did not start rich. So, when the Bible says, "Jesus became strong in spirit," it means that He was growing and maturing in spirit.

Now, the Holy Ghost was within Him from His birth. He was born of the Spirit of God, and yet—just like you and me— as He grew and matured, He had to start receiving the revelation of God's will out of His spirit so He could know the plan and will of God. Many people think that from six years old Jesus knew He was going to die on the cross. What kind of brutal, vicious Father would God be to bring a child here and from a very young age have Him know He is going to die? No, He grew. Just as He grew from the revelation of the Word and the Spirit of God within Him, you and I must grow in grace and favor by the revelation of the will and the Word of God within us. That is why you will not get saved one day and then have the total will of God come to pass in your life immediately on the next day. The reason is, you have not gotten the revelation of His will in your spirit; therefore, you have not yet started framing your world by the Word.

People who got saved yesterday want everything tomorrow. But the fact of the matter is that your tomorrows are the product of what you were speaking the days before you got saved. Remember this faith principle is a law, like the law of gravity. Whether you are saved or unsaved, you are receiving what you have been speaking. Through salvation God gives you access to the God-Kind of Faith. He says, "If you will start speaking My Word instead of your words, your world will start changing, and your circumstances will start coming into line with My will." Some of you right now have what you have been saying since being saved because you have not yet established the discipline of saying what God has said, instead of saying what your circumstance says.

Now, as He grew, Jesus was receiving the revelation of God's Word and God's will coming out of His spirit and illuminating His mind. Remember when Jesus was found in the temple at age twelve?

> So when they saw Him, they were amazed; and His mother said to Him, "Son, why have you done this to us? Look, Your father and I have sought You anxiously." And He said to them, "Why did you seek Me? Did you not know that I must be about My Father's business?" (Luke 2:48-49)

At age twelve, He was getting the revelation. What was deposited in His spirit was now coming to His mind, and His mind was coming into agreement with what was in His spirit. And He was saying, "You know what? I know now I am supposed to be about My Father's business. I did not know this at five, but I know it at twelve." This was someone who was growing in the knowledge of God's will. *"But they did not understand the statement which He spoke to them. Then He went down with them and came to Nazareth, and was subject to them, but His mother kept all these things in her heart. And Jesus increased in wisdom and stature, and in favor with God and men"* (Luke 2:50-52). Increasing in something means getting more than you had before. Notice, it says, "Jesus increased," not Christ. Christ is the inner man—the spirit on the inside of Jesus; but Jesus, the man (the natural man) increased.

From Jesus' age of twelve to the age of thirty is what many Bible scholars call "the silent years." The Gospel writers do not tell us anything about the life of Jesus from twelve to thirty. But the last picture that we see of Him at twelve—before He is baptized of John in the river Jordan at thirty—is this last statement: *"And Jesus increased in wisdom and stature, and in favor with God and men"* That means He was learning more about the plan of God, the will of God, and the purpose of God. He was learning more about who He was and what He was supposed to do. He was establishing the disciplines of a spiritual man so He could understand God's will and know how to walk in it.

The next time we see Him was when He came to John to be baptized of him at thirty years old. When John looked at Jesus, he said, *"Behold! The Lamb of God who takes away the sin of the world!"* (John 1:29) Jesus came to be baptized of John, and John said, *"I need to be baptized by You, and are You coming*

37

to me?" (Matthew 3:14) Jesus responded, *"Permit it to be so now, for thus it is fitting for us to fulfill all righteousness"* (Matthew 3:15). In other words, "I know who I am, and you know who I am; but the will of God has been revealed to Me, and this is necessary for Me to get into My purpose and My anointing. Between the years of twelve and thirty, the will of God for My life has been revealed to Me and this is a part of the will. So baptize Me, man, and let's get on with this!"

Now, at this point, Jesus was baptized the Spirit of the Lord descended upon Him in the form of a dove, and He began to walk in His earthly ministry. He performed no miracle before He was anointed with the Spirit of God. Until this baptism and anointing came upon Him, He did no miracle. Now, He was ready to begin His ministry and, between the ages of thirty and thirty-three, He began walking and doing all the things written in your Bible. The revelation of Jesus was revealed to Him by the Spirit and Word of God. He then began to know, "I am who the prophets have spoken of." He began to understand, "I am the Messiah, the one who is going to die for the sins of the world." He did not come into the earth knowing that, but at age thirty, He began to walk in it. He knew who He was. Therefore from age thirty to thirty-three, He was set toward the cross. He knew it. He had something amazing to accomplish—He was going to become sin for you and me, then He was going to die and be resurrected.

He began walking in the revelation of who He was and that He had something to accomplish. He had to do what no man had ever done before. He had to become sin, and He had to die, go into hell, pay for your sin and mine, and then come out of there with victory. No one had *ever* done this. A man was going to die, and in three days was going to be raised from the dead. Between the time that He died and gave up the Ghost on the cross, and the time that He came back into the body of Jesus (in Joseph of Arimathea's borrowed tomb), He was going into the lower parts of the earth and preach to the spirits in prison (see 1 Peter 3:19).

Jesus did not do this; Christ, the Anointed One and His anointing, did. The name of the flesh was *Jesus*. The name of the "greater one" on the inside was *Christ*. That's why He was called Jesus, the Christ—Christ was not Jesus' last name. That is why Isaiah 9:6 says, "*Unto us a Child is born, unto us a Son is given.*" The child Jesus was born flesh. The Son was not born; the Son was eternal with God. *"In the beginning was the Word, and the Word was with God, and the Word was God… and the Word became flesh"* (John 1:1,14). Christ was the name of the Word, and Jesus was the name given to the Word when God the Father gave Him a body. *"Sacrifice and offering You did not desire, but a body You have prepared for Me"* (Hebrews 10:5). Who was speaking if He did not have a body yet? "A body You have prepared for *Me, for Me!*" That was the Son—that was the Word.

On the cross, Jesus the flesh became sin and said, "*Eli, Eli, lama sabachthani?*" (Matthew 27:46) He was experiencing separation from God for the first time. Before the flesh expired, Christ said, *"Father, into Your hands I commit My spirit"* (Luke 23:46). The body of Jesus was laid in the tomb. Christ, the Anointed One, said, "Into Your hands I commit My spirit," not My flesh, My "spirit." So, the flesh went into the tomb and the spirit went into the hands of the Father to accomplish the will of God.

Beyond Personal Power

First Peter 3:19 tells us "...*He went and preached to the spirits in prison.*" Ephesians 4:9 says, "*Now this, 'He ascended'— what does it mean but that He also first descended into the lower parts of the earth?*" By the time He went to the cross, He knew that the plan of redemption and the condition of the entire world was dependent upon His fulfilling this assignment. And He had to do it, not as God but as a man anointed with the Spirit of God. Today, you may be saying, "God has given me an impossible task. He is telling me to do something that no one has ever done before. How can He expect me to do it?" Because Jesus did it! And if you will do as Jesus did, you will also be able to do what no other man has ever done before, if you use the God-Kind of Faith.

So, what did Jesus do? He became fully knowledgeable and fully persuaded of God's Word. He was looking into the Word of God from age twelve to thirty, finding out what the prophets said. He was reading Isaiah and Jeremiah. He was studying the law of Moses—Genesis, Exodus, Leviticus, Numbers, and Deuteronomy, and seeing the pattern of Himself. He was reading David and discerned that the written Word was talking about Him. You begin to walk in power when you start looking into that Word and find out that "it is talking about me."

He read in Isaiah 53:5: "*He was wounded for our transgressions, He was bruised for our iniquities; the chastisement for our peace was upon Him, and by His stripes we are healed.*" As He was reading it, the Spirit of God said, "That's about You!" One day, at about eighteen or nineteen years old, perhaps He looked over Deuteronomy 18:15 where Moses said: "*The Lord your God will raise up for you a Prophet like me from your midst, from your brethren. Him you shall hear."* And the Spirit of God said, "That's about You." He was reading where the Bible says: *"For He shall grow up before Him as a tender...root out of dry ground"* (Isaiah 53:2), and *"That I will raise to David a Branch of righteousness..."* (Jeremiah 23:5), and God said, "That's You." So, Jesus began to walk with this knowledge.

Many of us want to do ministry and do great things for God. We receive the anointing of the Holy Ghost, but we have not taken the years "between twelve and thirty yet," and we are wondering why God isn't using us as we desire to be used. Do you know why? It is because we have not yet established the discipline to frame our world by the Word of God. When situations come to us, we say the first thing that comes into our mind instead of what is already in our spirit—you cannot do ministry like that.

In Matthew 16, Peter at Caesarea Philippi had confessed that Jesus was the Christ. One of His disciples finally knew who He was by the Spirit of God. Jesus asked them:

"Who do men say that I, the Son of Man, am?" So they said, "Some say John the Baptist, some Elijah, and others Jeremiah or one of the prophets." He said to them, "But who do you say that I am?" Simon Peter answered and said, "You are the Christ, the Son of the living God" (Matthew 16:13-16).

Because most of us are not of Hebrew origin, we do not understand the power of the revelation when Peter said, "You are the Anointed One." What he was saying is, "You are the One whom all the prophets have told us was coming; that is who You are. You are the One of whom Isaiah, Jeremiah,

Beyond Personal Power

Ezekiel, Daniel, Hosea, Habakkuk, and all the prophets spoke." *"From that time Jesus began to show to His disciples that He must go to Jerusalem, and suffer many things from the elders and chief priests and scribes, and be killed, and be raised the third day"* (Matthew 16:21). "From that time" means He was not saying this before, but from that time He started saying, "You know what, I am going to go to Jerusalem, I am going to die, and I am going to be raised from the dead."

"You are going to get what you say, not what you pray."

Now, notice what Peter did when He said this: *"Then Peter took Him aside and began to rebuke Him, saying, 'Far be it from You, Lord; this shall not happen to You!' But He turned and said to Peter, 'Get behind Me, Satan! You are an offense to Me, for you are not mindful of the things of God, but the things of men'"* (Matthew 16:22-23). Why was He saying that? It was because Peter did not understand what Jesus was doing. **Jesus was speaking the Word of God that He had to speak in order to be raised from the dead**. Because the God-Kind of Faith speaks what it believes based on the Word of God, you have to tell anything that will keep you from speaking God's Word to "get behind you." Look at those people and say, "You do not understand what I am doing; I have to do this to get God's results. I am not just speaking. This is the way I am going to get out of this. This is the way I am going to do and finish what everybody says cannot happen! This is how I am going to accomplish what nobody has ever accomplished before! I have to take what God has said to me and say it!"

Jesus rebuked Peter because Jesus was putting into effect the principle of the God-Kind of Faith, and without that,

42

Speak What You Believe

there would have been no resurrection. If He had not said it, it would not have come to pass. You need to hear what I am telling you. He had to live just like you—He was your example. When you know you are about to die in the natural, you must start declaring what God has said. You need to tell anything that would keep you from doing that, to "get behind me, get out of my house and out of my way. Sorry, I cannot hang out with you anymore because you are ruining my resurrection." The resurrection came to pass because Jesus exercised the God-Kind of Faith. We must destroy the religious spirit that we have been under that makes us think the plans of God are automatic. It was not even automatic for Jesus. In Mark 11:23-24, Jesus said, *"Whoever says and...believes that those things He says will be done, he will have whatever he says. Therefore I say to you, whatever things you ask when you pray, believe that you receive them, and you will have them."* He said you are not going to get what you **pray;** you are going to get what you **say**.

> *For assuredly, I say to you, whoever says to this mountain, "Be removed and be cast into the sea," and does not doubt in his heart, but believes that those things he says will be done, he will have whatever he says* (Mark 11:23).

That is why I am telling you whatsoever you desire when you pray, believe you receive. I am telling you to believe you receive when you pray, because you are not going to get what you pray, you are going to get what you say. I am telling you to believe that you receive when you pray, so that right after you pray, you will say, "I have what I just prayed for." When you say, "I have what I just prayed for," you will have what you say because you do not get what you pray, you get what you say.

43

(Read these lines again!) That is why a lot of people pray for things but do not receive. After they pray for it, they do not say, "I have it." Your saying and your praying are not in agreement—*You do not get what you pray; you get what you say.*

Only when what you say is in alignment with what you pray will you see it come to pass or manifested with regularity. Putting this principle into effect assured Jesus of the resurrection. It was the will of God for Him to die and be resurrected, but just because it was God's will did not mean it was going to happen. As the Word of God was revealed to Him, Jesus grew in the knowledge that He was going to die and be raised again the third day. He began to put into effect the vital principle of faith—speaking what He believed!

Jesus had to exercise His faith to be resurrected. It was the will of God, but the will of God does not have to be done in the earth unless someone exercises their faith. The will of God will not be done in your life—even though you know it—if you do not exercise your faith because the will of God is not automatic. People think, "Well, once I know God's will, everything will be all right." No, everything will not be all right. If you do not exercise your faith, you can know God's will and miss it by a thousand miles.

The will of God does not come because somebody knows it; the will of God comes because somebody says, "Thy kingdom come, Thy will be done, in earth as it is in Heaven." Jesus says, "Say it." If you do not say it, you will not see it. You, as a believer, need to understand this because some of us have been going to church for twenty years saying, "I need to know the will of God." Read the Book and start speaking that Word! In John 10:17, Jesus was speaking before the cross:

> *Therefore My Father loves Me, because I lay down My life that I may take it again. No one takes it from Me, but I lay it down of Myself. I have power to lay it down, and I have power to take it again. This command I have received from My Father* (John 10:17-18).

He was saying, "No man takes My life; I lay it down. It may look like the Sanhedrin, Pilate, and the Romans are in control, but understand that this is a setup and nobody takes My life from Me—I lay it down of Myself." In other words, "I have power to lay it down, and I have power to pick it up. *I am saying this because God said it to Me, and, I am saying it before I get betrayed, before I go before Pilate, before I hang on the cross, and before I give up the Ghost; because if I do not say it, it is not going to happen.*" See, if you do not speak God's Word concerning your circumstance, God's will *will not* come to pass in your life. It is God's will for you to be healed, prospered, and delivered, but just because it is God's will does not mean it is going to happen. It is not going to happen until you get the Word in your mouth and start speaking that Word into your future.

> *Therefore My Father loves Me, because I lay down My life that I may take it again. No one takes it from Me, but I lay it down of Myself. I have power to lay it down, and I have power to take it again. This command I have received from My Father* (John 10:17-18).

Before He was betrayed, before He went to Pilate, and before the Sanhedrin condemned Him to death, Jesus said that nobody was taking His life; rather, that He laid it down on His own. *"I have the power to lay it down, and I have the power to take it up again. This commandment I received from My Father."* First of all, He wants you to understand that nobody was taking His life, but He was laying it down. Secondly, He said, "I want you to know that I have the power to lay it down, and I have the power to pick it up again." When He said, "I have the power to lay it down, and I have the power to take it up again," at that moment He did not have the power. He was going to need the power after that; but because He understood the vital principle of faith, and because He had the mental disposition of faith—that speaks what it believes in the present tense—He said, "I have the power," not "I'm going to have" or "I will have." He said, "I have the power *now* to lay it down, and I have the power *now* to pick it up again."

Let me demonstrate what I mean by saying, "He did not have the power when He first said it." Remember when Jesus went to the Garden of Gethsemane where He wrestled with the will of God being done in His life for the first time? He said, "Father, if there is any other way to get this done without Me dying, let this cup pass. If We can do this any other way, let Us do it another way." That does not sound like somebody who has the power! Not yet! He, like many of us, was trying to find an alternative means of getting the will of God done; He was trying to do it another way, just like we do. He was wrestling with His flesh, but because He had already said, "I have the power," when He got into the situation where He needed the power, His confession met Him. This is what the life of faith does.

The Bible says, *"He sent His word"* (Psalm 107:20). You have to get that Word and send it into your future. The life of faith is the kind of life that is always running into its confessions. It says today, "All my needs are met," not "All my needs will be met." And when it comes up against a situation of lack, it runs into its confession. When the bank account says, "It is not going to happen this time," the Word says, "Oh no, he already sent the Word into this." I am running into my confessions all the time. Because I am a man of faith, when I run into it, and I need the power, I have it!

He says, "I have the power *now* to lay it down, and I have the power to pick it up again. This commandment I have received from My Father." He was saying that what He was speaking right now was what God had said. He said, "I have the power to lay it down, and I have the power to pick it up again, and the reason I am saying this now is because God's Word said it to Me." So, He was speaking God's Word to Himself in the present tense; the power He needed was available to Him when He came into the circumstance where He needed it because He had already said, "I have it." (Read this paragraph again.)

So when He went into the garden and wrestled, He said, "Father, if there is any other way to get this done, let Us find another way. And He went back again, "Father, let this cup pass." And He went back a third time, "Father, if there is any way to do this without all this pain and suffering, can We do it another way? Nevertheless...." (That is where the power kicked in). "Not My will, but Thy will."

You can go once, twice, or three times trying to live this Christian life another way. You can try everything your mind thinks you should do. You can try to figure it out on your own ability, taking all your intellect and education to try to get God's will done in your life, but it is not going to happen that way. The only way it is going to happen is when you do what Jesus did. If Jesus had to live that way, then there is no way in the world you are going to see the God-Kind of results any other way. You have to get God's Word in your mouth, His promise concerning your future, and start saying, "I have it. I have it. I am not going to get it; I have it now." But you are saying, "Bishop, I do not see it now." That is right; you do not see it now, **but you have it now. And if you say that you have it now, you will see it later!**

God the Father had to do this very same thing to raise Jesus from the dead. Not only did Jesus exercise the God-Kind of Faith in His earthly life and ministry, and even towards His resurrection, but God the Father also exercised the principle of faith in resurrecting Jesus from the dead. Now, what is our objective here? If Jesus had to exercise the God-Kind of Faith in order for the will of God to be manifested in His life, and if the Father had to exercise the God-Kind of Faith to produce His will in the earth, then there is no way that you and I, as children of God, can see the God-Kind of results and live the God-Kind of life if we do not put into effect the God-Kind of Faith.

Earlier we established that the Bible's definition of faith is different from religion's definition of faith. Since God the Father is the One who said, *"The just shall live by faith"* and *"Without faith, it is impossible to please Him,"* then we better know what He says faith is, and not what our momma, daddy, or preacher says it is. God's Word establishes some significant truths regarding Bible Faith.

Remember that according to James 2, Bible Faith is "conviction or persuasion plus corresponding action." It is not Bible Faith until your conviction or persuasion has a corresponding action—something that can be seen or heard. Faith also has a vital principle and a mental disposition: Faith is always present tense.

> *"It is not Bible faith until your conviction has a corresponding action—something that can be seen or heard."*

Bible Faith takes the promises of God and speaks them in the present tense. So, if faith speaks what it believes, then the God-Kind of Faith speaks *God's Word* in the present tense. Only the believer has access to that level of faith because the unbeliever does not have the authority to use God's Word. When Jesus said, "Whatever you ask in My name," it did not mean whatever you ask and attach His name to. The Greek word for *name* is *onoma*, and it means "nature, character and authority." Here, Jesus was saying, "Whatever you ask in My nature because *you* have a right to My nature. Whatever you ask in My authority because *you*, as My child, have a right to My authority; whatever you ask in My character because *you*, as My blood-bought child, have a right to My character." Therefore, *you* have a right to a higher level of faith more than anybody else. I made up my mind that since I have the right to it, that I am going to use it. Remember the earlier example of my cars? A Dodge Omni and a Rolls Royce are both cars, but one gets you to your destination at another level, at another speed, and in another environment.

Again, *the God-Kind of Faith is the kind of faith that speaks God's Word in the present tense in response to circumstances and situations.* If there is someone who does not want the Jesus-Kind of results, check them out and move away from them because they will contaminate you with their negativity and unbelief. If you and I are going to walk in the God-Kind of Faith, we will have to discipline ourselves to make sure that what comes out of our mouths in response to circumstances and situations is the living Word of God. You cannot just say anything you want to say. You have to put a guard over your mouth. You have to be quick to hear and slow to speak. You cannot say, "Well, I don't know, I think I am going to go under." If you say that, then you are going to go under because you will have what you say. But, if you get God's Word in your mouth and say, "Greater is He that is in me than he that is in the world," and then declare, "This is the victory that overcomes the world, even my faith, and I am walking by faith, and I have faith," you will start overcoming. You are not supposed to be going under. You are supposed to be overcoming.

God calls you an "over-comer." An over-comer *comes over*; he does not go under. Everyone has an opportunity to go under, but the over-comer chooses not to go under. He chooses to go over because he speaks God's Word in the present tense. Remember when Jesus saw the fig tree He said, "*Let no one eat fruit from you ever again,*" and Mark 11:14 says, "**In response**, *Jesus said to it….*" The barrenness of the fig tree was communicating to Him, and in response, He spoke the Word of God. This is what you have to do: You have to meet your lack, fear, or sickness with a godly response. You must respond and make sure that what you are saying is the Word of the living God. Jesus put this principle into effect in His life, even regarding the resurrection from the dead, as the will of God was revealed to Him. You must holler back!

On earth, Jesus lived as a man anointed with the Holy Ghost. So He did everything, not because He was Jesus, but because the power of the Holy Spirit was upon and within Him—just like the power of the Holy Spirit is upon and within you. He is our example. Just as He had to exercise His faith for the will of God to come to pass in His life, you and I also must exercise our faith.

I mentioned earlier that God the Father actually exercised this very principle in resurrecting Jesus from the dead. Hebrews chapter 1 takes us into the heavens during the time that Jesus had died and gone into the lower parts of the earth. Jesus had died on the cross and Christ, the Anointed One and His anointing, was being given back into the hands of the Father.

The Spirit went into the hands of the Father, and the flesh went into Joseph's tomb. Now, what happened in those three days? Look at verse 18 of First Peter chapter 3: "*For Christ also suffered once for sins, the just for the unjust, that He might bring us to God, being put to death in the flesh, but made alive by the Spirit.*" Who suffered? Christ did, not Jesus. Now, "*the just*" means He had never sinned; but He suffered for us—the unjust who had sinned—because the Bible says that on the cross "*He that knew no sin was made to be sin.*" Understand, Jesus never committed sin, but He became sin on the cross.

Beyond Personal Power

God laid on Him the iniquity of us all and the flesh was put to death, but His spirit was made alive by the Holy Spirit.

His soul was made an offering for sin (see Isaiah 53:10). That means His soul died, for *"the wages of sin is death"* and death is separation from God. *"By whom also He went and preached to the spirits in prison"* (1 Peter 3:19). What prison? The prison in which the spirits of just men were held until redemption's price was paid because no one could get into Heaven until redemption's price was paid in full. So, for every man in the Old Covenant who died in faith believing that a Messiah would come, there was a place where those spirits were held. Jesus called it "Abraham's bosom." It was a matter of spiritual legality.

The Bible says that when the rich man died he lifted up his eyes in hell and looked and saw the beggar in "Abraham's bosom" (see Luke 16:23). That was not Heaven. You cannot see Heaven from hell, and you cannot see hell from Heaven. Heaven would not be a glorious place if you could see the torment of your loved ones who died.

Abraham was the father of faith, and this was a place where the faithful were held. I am not talking about purgatory, which the Bible does not say anything about; it was called Abraham's bosom.

> *He was oppressed and He was afflicted, yet He opened not His mouth; He was led as a lamb to the slaughter, and as a sheep before its shearers is silent, so He opened not His mouth. He was taken from prison and from judgment, and who will declare His generation?...Yet it pleased the Lord to bruise Him; He has put Him to grief.* **When you make His**

soul an offering for sin, He shall see His seed, He shall prolong His days, and the pleasure of the Lord shall prosper in His hand. He shall see the labor of His soul, and be satisfied (Isaiah 53:7-8,10-11).

Isaiah was saying that it pleased God the Father to bruise Him and make *His* soul an offering for sin. Now, the wages of sin is death. So, if Jesus' soul was made an offering for sin, then Jesus' soul experienced death or separation from God. He died in a state of sin, not because He committed it, but because He became sin on the cross. He took yours and mine.

Now, any soul that dies in a state of sin must go to hell. This bothers some people to say that Jesus went to hell; but if He did not, then you and I have to go there because that is part of the full price of redemption. Paying the price meant He had to pay it all. So, God made His soul an offering for sin. In other words, the Father was watching Jesus be made sin, going into the lower parts of the earth and paying the price for our sin, which means He—like every other soul that dies in a state of sin—was held captive in hell by Satan and his demons. Now, this is what your Savior did for you. The Father was watching to see what Christ would endure, and when *He* saw Him suffer in hell for your sin and mine, the Father said, "I am satisfied. The price for sin is paid in full." *"By His knowledge My righteous Servant shall justify many"* (Isaiah 53:11). In other words, He went to justify many by what He did because He put this principle of faith into effect.

Remember, Jesus had to go to hell and come back, and no one had ever done that before. The Father told *Him*, "You have got to go and pay for sin, but You are coming back," **and**

Jesus had to believe it, even though it had never been done before. That is why He said before He went, "Nobody takes My life; I lay it down. I have the power to lay it down, and I have the power to pick it up. I am saying this because My Father said it to Me; and if I do not say it, it will not happen." He made *His* soul an offering for sin and the Father saw it and was satisfied.

Ephesians 4 puts together pieces of a puzzle that the Bible very clearly paints, but because it does not paint it all in one place, most Christians do not know it. The principle is "*Here a little, there a little, line upon line, precept upon precept*" (Isaiah 28:10). Look at Ephesians 4:7-8, "*But to each one of us grace was given according to the measure of Christ's gift.*" Therefore He says: "*When He ascended on high, He led captivity captive.*" In other words, He took those who had been keeping souls captive and made them His captive. He took their authority from them.

Then He said, "Now, you are My captive, because all authority in heaven and earth has been given to Me" (see Matthew 28:18). Look at Ephesians 4:9: " '*He ascended'—what does it mean but that He also first descended into the lower parts of the earth? He who descended is also the One who ascended far above all the heavens, that He might fill all things.*" If He had to fill all things, that means He had to go into the lower parts of the earth—into hell—and come out. *You cannot give people authority over that which you have not established authority over.* So, for Jesus to give you and me authority over devils and demons, He had to first establish that authority. He did not do it by sending a memo or electronic mail (e-mail). He did that when He became sin. His soul was made an offering for sin and—like every other soul that dies in a state of sin—He went into the lower parts of the earth. And just like every other soul that dies in a state of separation from God, He was held captive by Satan. The demons grabbed hold of Him, saying, "You thought You were the Son of God; You thought You would get out of here. You are just like everybody else."

However, we speak wisdom among those who are mature, yet not the wisdom of this age, nor of the rulers of this age, who are coming to nothing. But we speak the wisdom of God in a mystery, the hidden wisdom which God ordained before the ages for our glory, which none of the rulers of this age knew; for had they known, they would not have crucified the Lord of glory (1 Corinthians 2:6-8).

If the demons, devils, Pilate, and the Jews knew this, then they would not have crucified Him. In Isaiah 53:10, the Bible says that the Father will see it, *"and shall see the labor of His soul."* In other words, when He sees Christ wrestle for His freedom in hell, *He* will be satisfied.

God, who at various times and in various ways spoke in time past to the fathers by the prophets, has in these last days spoken to us by His Son, whom He has appointed heir of all things, through whom also He made the worlds; who being the brightness of His glory and the express image of His person, and upholding all things by the word of His power, when He had by Himself purged our sins, sat down at the right hand of the Majesty on high, having become so much better than the angels, as He has by inheritance obtained a more excellent name than they. For to which of the angels did He ever say: "You are My Son, Today I have begotten You"? (Hebrews 1:1-5)

He has obtained a more excellent name by inheritance, so He did not get this more excellent name until after death. He died in a state lower than angels (human); after He purged our sins, He was raised in a state better than angels, higher in authority than angels. Demons are fallen angels. Notice that He is saying this, *"To which of the angels did He ever say…?"* The answer is that God never said this to any of the angels, so who did He say it to? Here the Scripture is showing you what the Father said to the Son during the time that the Son was purging our sins. This is God, by the Holy Spirit, taking you into Heaven during the time of the crucifixion and showing you what was happening up there. Jesus was already begotten of the Holy Ghost and His earthly mother Mary in Nazareth (see Luke 1:26-38), but the Scripture says that "when He is making His soul a sacrifice" (when He is purging our sin), the Father leans over the battlements of Heaven, looks down into hell and says, *"You are My Son, **today**, I have begotten You* [or, I am birthing You today]." That means He was dead in sin, having paid for my sin and yours, **and the Father births Him again**. In other words, He said He will be a Father to Him again: *"I will be to Him a Father, and He shall be to Me a Son"* (Hebrews 1:5).

Christ, the Anointed One, was in hell to purge our sins. The Father saw it and His soul was satisfied. The demons were saying, "You are here, You have to stay here, and You are not coming out." But Jesus had already said, "I have the power to lay it down, and I have the power to take it up again." The Father saw the Son struggling to get out, but He could not. He saw the labor of His soul, and when the Father had seen enough and was satisfied that your sin and my sin had been purged and paid for, the Father leaned over and said, **"You are *My* Son, today I have begotten You."**

"But when He again brings the firstborn into the world, He says, 'Let all the angels of God worship Him' " (Hebrews 1:6). "He brings the firstborn into the world *again*," means He did it once in Bethlehem and He was doing it again; He was called "the firstborn," not "the only begotten." Why? Because He was the first of millions of others who are going to be released just like this—by the Word! Jesus, the Christ was *born again.* When the Father said, *"Let all the angels of God worship Him"* (Hebrew 1:6), that Word went down into hell and the devils had to turn Him loose because demons are fallen angels.

Jesus would not have been resurrected if He had not spoken God's Word before He went to the cross and if the Father had not spoken His Word as He watched Christ suffer captivity for our sins. You will not see the will of God in the earth unless *you say so!* It was the will of the Father that the Son come back justified, glorious, and powerful; but it was not going to happen just because the Father willed it—it was going to happen only when the *Father spoke it.*

When He had seen the sacrifice and it was acceptable, He said, "Enough is enough! Let all the angels of God worship Him," and Christ was released from those demon hands. He—now being a justified, born-again spirit—went over to Satan in hell and said, "I believe you have something that belongs to Me. I want the keys to *death* now, and I want the keys to *hell* because you no longer have power over either one. You do not have power over death, and you can no longer send anyone to hell. If they choose to live by faith, they can be free." God does not send anyone to hell and the devil does not send you to hell. The devil does not have power to send anyone to hell. Only *you* have power to send *you* to hell, and you do that by what does or does not come out of your mouth. *"If you confess with your mouth the Lord Jesus and believe in your heart that God has*

"The God-Kind of Faith speaks the Word of God."

raised Him from the dead, you will be saved" (Romans 10:9).

He went from there and *"He led captivity captive"* (Ephesians 4:8). He unlocked the place holding the souls of just men who died in faith believing a Messiah was coming, and said, "Boys, it's time to get out of here." Ephesians says, *"He led captivity captive."* On His way back to glory, He stopped by Joseph's tomb and slipped back into the body named *Jesus*—a body that was so destroyed on the cross by beatings and whippings that it was indistinguishable.

The Old Testament says, *"So His visage was marred more than any man"* (Isaiah 52:14). He went back into that body, and when this resurrected spirit struck, that body was completely restored. Life came back to it and emanated from it so that stones had to move. He then appeared and said, *"All authority has been given to Me in heaven and on earth"* (Matthew 28:18). This is for you to see and understand that the will of God was done in Jesus' life by His speaking the Word of God. The Father's will was accomplished in our justification by speaking His Word. If Jesus and the Father had to speak the Word, what makes you think that you are going to see God's will in your life without speaking the Word of God?

Speak What You Believe

Notice, the Father did not say, "All the angels are going to worship Him." He said, "Let all the angels worship Him." The inference in the latter statement is "now" because faith *is* always *present tense*. Child of God, this is how resurrection occurs in your life. This is how healing happens in your life. This is how the power of God is released into the circumstances of your life. Someone says, "I am waiting for God to intervene." God says, "The Word is in your mouth and in your heart." You are waiting on God to show up and He is waiting on you to speak it. You are waiting for God to heal you and He is waiting for you to declare His Word, "By His stripes, I am healed." You are waiting for God to meet your need and He is waiting for you to put His Word in your mouth and declare, "My God has supplied all of my need according to His riches in glory by Christ Jesus." You are waiting for someone to give you some money, and after you have tithed and given offerings, God is waiting for you to declare "that it is being given to me again, good measure, pressed down, shaken together, and running over, men *are* giving into my bosom."

My purpose is to help you see from God's Word how this is done. So at least, if you choose not to live this way, you will know why God's will is not being accomplished in your life. If you do not start speaking God's Word instead of whatever you want to say concerning the situation or the attacks or what is lacking in your life, the situation is not going to change. God does not want you broke, sick, bound, sad, sorrowful, angry, or addicted. He wants you saved, healed, prospered, delivered, and set free. But He says, "I can only work with My Word." Someone might ask, "But Bishop, isn't

59

God with me everywhere?" Absolutely! But He is not manifesting His will everywhere.

The Father gave us a look at that in the Book of Genesis, where the Bible says, "*In the beginning, the Spirit of God was hovering over the face of the waters*" (Genesis 1:2). The Spirit of God was present, but nothing happened until God spoke, "Let there be light." **When He spoke, the Spirit of God moved with the Word of God to manifest the will of God**. The Spirit of God is present with you right now. He has been with you and around you—He has never left you. He has not left, no matter what you have been doing. But He cannot move until somebody speaks His Word. When His Word is spoken, the Spirit of God goes into operation to bring that Word to pass.

Chapter 4

Fight the Faith Fight

Chapter 4

Fight the Faith Fight

———

Faith is a lifestyle, not a trend or a fad. It is not something that you can do for a couple of weeks and then stop and say, "This is not working." It is a lifestyle. You will be amazed once you begin to put the Word of God in your mouth.

An important element of Bible Faith is found in First Timothy 6:12, which reads, *"Fight the good fight of faith, lay hold on eternal life, to which you were also called and have confessed the good confession in the presence of many witnesses."* You

"Faith is a lifestyle." must understand that it is a faith fight. You and I are involved in a fight for our faith. The Scripture tells us that we are to *"fight the good fight of faith."* This is the only place in the New Testament where you and I are told to fight. The fight that you and I are involved in is for our faith. We are not called to fight devils. We are not called to fight demons. We are not called to fight people. We are not called to fight brothers and sisters. We are not called to fight preachers. We are called to fight the fight of faith. Literally, we are called to fight for our faith. When the Bible says in verse 12, *"Fight the good fight of faith,"* it is literally telling you that the fight is for your faith, and if you are going to win, then you have to maintain your faith.

> *"If we are to act like God, then we are to respond to circumstances and situations like He does— speak His Word and change the circumstances."*

Although the Bible says in Ephesians 6:12 that *"we do not wrestle against flesh and blood, but against principalities, against powers…,"* it is important to note that it does not say that we fight. There is a difference between a fight and a wrestle. The writer did not say that we fight with powers and principalities. He says *"we wrestle not against flesh and blood."* But again, we wrestle; we do not fight. You are not called to fight the devil. You do not have power to fight him. You do not have authority to fight him. Jesus did not give you authority to fight the devil. Jesus gave you authority to cast him out. A lot of people lose their battle with the devil because they are trying to fight him instead of casting him out. You are not graced to carry on conversations with the devil. That is why you will lose if you get into an argument with a devil.

You are not anointed to argue with the devil. You are anointed to cast him out. You cannot get into an argument with a demon and win. If a child of God gets into an argument with the devil, you know what starts happening—you start acting like a devil because he pulls you out of your anointing. So understand that you and I are not graced to argue and converse with demons. Jesus said to cast them out.

The only place that you and I are instructed to fight is in this area—for our faith. It is a faith fight. The enemy is after our faith. The enemy is not after you. You are flesh and blood. He is not really interested in sending

"It is a faith fight."

you to hell. That is not his objective. Once you are in hell, you are no problem to him. He feels no victory by bringing or taking you to hell. His objective is to neutralize your effectiveness on this planet. He is not trying to get you to hell. You are forgotten once you are in hell. You are a captive and you are not leaving and God did not send you there.

As a matter of fact, if one goes to hell, one goes there because he or she lost the fight of faith because you never confessed Jesus Christ as Lord! It never came out of your mouth that Jesus is Lord, to the glory of God. You never got around to speaking your confession of faith. Your whole life Satan kept you from making that one confession and that is his objective. His objective is keeping you from making that one confession. And if you do make that one, then he works overtime, double-time, triple-time to get you in some religious mausoleum where that is the only Word that you ever confess. He wants you some place where you never begin to confess the Word about healing or prosperity because it is a faith fight.

Remember in James chapter 2, the biblical definition of faith is **conviction or persuasion plus corresponding action**. We also have come to understand that faith has a vital principle. The vital principle of faith is that faith speaks what it believes. Speaking the Word of God is vital or the primary act of faith. If we are to fight the good fight of faith, then what the Bible is telling us is that your fight and my fight is to keep our conviction and our corresponding action, which is the speaking of the Word of God, in our mouth continually. That is what the fight is. *Every attack, every distraction, everything that the enemy hits you with is to get you to stop speaking the Word of God*, and to stop causing your conviction and your corresponding action to agree. That is the fight. That is the fight of faith.

The enemy knows that you are of no danger to him if he can separate you from your faith. If he can separate you from your conviction or persuasion plus your corresponding action, if he can get you to shut up and to stop speaking the Word of God or if he can get you in such a place where you are so cognizant of your circumstance, your situation, and your lack to where you say, "You know what? This does not work; I am going to stop speaking the Word of God," then he knows that he has you. He knows this. It is a faith fight.

Once you learn this and you understand the faith-fear connection, you will see how much of a faith fight it really is. Faith and fear are connected. They are two different ends of the same rope. Fear actually is faith. It is just the other end of faith. The faith fight is a fight for what is coming out of your mouth. Most Christians believe God's Word—if they ever read it or if someone ever speaks it to them. The problem is that we do not understand that believing or conviction alone is not faith and we think that because "I believe this" then it should be happening. No, it is not going to happen until your believing or conviction or persuasion is coupled with a *corresponding action*, and the vital corresponding action is speaking what you believe.

Faith-Fear Connection

Again, when we talk about Bible Faith, we are really talking about the biblical definition of faith, not your definition or religion's definition. Looking through our various texts, we have discovered that the Bible tells us that faith is "conviction or persuasion plus corresponding action," which means that believing by itself is not faith. Faith is only that which can be seen or heard. I realize that we have established this truth on several different levels, but it is especially important when you are dealing with the faith-fear connection.

It is a faith fight and you must understand the faith-fear connection. First Timothy 6:12 reads: *"Fight the good fight of faith, lay hold on eternal life, to which you were also called and have confessed the good confession in the presence of many witnesses."* Again, you and I are involved in a fight for our faith. In fact, it is the only fight that the Bible tells us as believers to fight.

The Bible says in Ephesians 6:12 that, *"We wrestle not against flesh and blood, but against principalities, against powers...."* That is to say that we wrestle against demonic forces. However, I say again that we are not called to fight demonic forces—we are called to fight the fight of faith because the enemy is after your faith. His desire is *not* to make you feel bad or to make you sick. The enemy desires your faith because our faith is the only thing that makes you and I dangerous to him. And if he can get your faith, then he knows that he has your victory.

First John 5:4 says: *"For whatever is born of God overcomes the world. And this is the victory that has overcome the world—our faith."* When the Bible says this, it does not mean that you will overcome simply because you are born of God. We mistakenly think that because we are Christians, we will overcome. God says, "No, that is not so. The victory that overcomes the world [or the way to overcome] is by faith." **The implication is that what is born of God has His nature and His character, and therefore, acts like Him**. If we are to act like God, then we are to respond to circumstances and situations like He does— speak His Word and change the circumstances. You will not overcome simply because you are born again.

I know religion has taught us that we will win every victory because we are blood-washed and our name is written in the Lamb's Book of Life, but that is simply our registration. It's what gives us the legal rights to speak God's Word! If you do not discipline yourself to exercise your faith by getting the Word of God in your mouth, then you can be saved and still defeated for the rest of your earthly life because it is a faith fight.

Faith has nothing to do with your emotions. Faith is outside the realm of emotions. Faith is not just believing and it is not emotional. It is an *act that co-responds*, or an action that answers back to what you say it is that you believe. Again, speaking is the primary act of faith. It is the first one. You will not do other acts if you do not first do that one.

Look at Second Corinthians 5:7 where the Bible says, "*For we walk by faith, not by sight.*" If we put our working definition for faith in the verse, it reads: "*For we walk by conviction or persuasion plus corresponding actions, not by sight.*" A more accurate word for "sight" would be *senses*. God is not referring to visual perception here. If that were the case, then it would be okay to walk by touch or by one of the other senses. The walk of faith is a walk that leaves the realm of the senses. It does not ignore the senses; it simply does not speak what the senses tell it.

Beyond Personal Power

Again, we walk by faith and not by sight. We all know that to walk is to move forward. God tells you and I how to move forward—that is, how to get from where you are to where His Word says you are supposed to be. You will not get there by attending church. You will not get there by being a bishop, elder, or deacon. You get there when you learn to discipline yourself—to cause your conviction and your corresponding action to line up.

"Faith has nothing to do with your emotions. Faith is outside the realm of emotions."

Remember that the vital principle of faith is that "faith speaks what it believes." Therefore, you move forward by believing (conviction or persuasion) plus speaking what you believe (corresponding action) because this is the vital principle of faith. God gave it to me like this: You have a rope, and we will call this rope "Bible Faith," or conviction or persuasion plus corresponding action—it is a rope of faith. On one end of the rope we have what is called the "God-Kind of Faith," as Jesus instructed in Mark 11:22-24 to *"have faith in God,"* which again means the God-Kind of Faith or the brand of faith that God has. It is the kind of faith to which only the believer has access. That is why you were born again—so you could have access to the God-Kind of Faith.

If faith speaks what it believes and the believer believes the Word of God, then the God-Kind of Faith is the kind that speaks the Word of God. This is the kind of faith that Jesus commanded you and I as a believer to have. What I want you to see is that on one end of the rope is the God-Kind of Faith (see Mark 11:22-24), and on the other side of the rope is another "brand of faith" called fear.

In the same way faith is not an emotion, neither is fear. It is the same spiritual force. The faith life is a life that does not believe what its senses are saying, but it believes what the Word of God says regardless of what it looks or smells like.

"Fear is faith because just like faith, fear speaks what it believes. The problem with fear is that what fear believes is not the truth!"

That is why the assault on your senses is so great. That is why in order to walk by faith, there are some things that you cannot hear or listen to, some people you cannot hang out with, some movies you should not see. It is not because seeing the movie is a sin, but because that particular movie may affect your faith.

Fear is faith (conviction or persuasion plus corresponding action) in the wrong set of realities. It is faith in your experience: You have been in this place before and you know how it turned out so you believe that it will turn out like that again. Therefore, you speak how it turned out before, and God calls that *fear*.

Fear is faith in your negative reinforcement. For example, your mom and your grandma had the very same condition the doctor says is now afflicting you, and because they died from it, you believe it. You believe it based on the previous experiences of someone else and you do not even know why you believe it. Most of the time, you do not even realize that you believe it, but you know that you believe it because you have been speaking it. *Fear is faith in your opinion.*

69

Beyond Personal Power

It is impossible to walk by faith without information—so you received the information from somewhere. You must understand that you have been receiving information from the time you were born. It is fallen and unredeemed information. God is trying to give you redeemed information. That is why you must watch from where you get your information!

"Divine Principle: Fear is faith in the wrong set of realities."

The Bible's definition of faith is not an emotion and its definition of fear is not an emotion. This is why Jesus says, "*...does not doubt in his heart, but believes...*" (Mark 11:23). He did not say "in your mind" because your mind may be full of questions, but that does not mean that you doubt in your heart. God knows that you are not doubting in your heart because the Bible says, "*For with the heart one believes unto righteousness, and with the mouth confession is made unto salvation*" (Romans 10:10). It does not say, "With the heart, man tries to believe." In other words, whatever man believes, he speaks. You believe what gets on the inside of you.

Fear is also an action because it is on the other end of faith. *Fear also has a vital principle: It is not fear until you speak it.* Do you understand that you can be crazy on the inside, but just like it is not faith on the inside of you, neither is it fear on the inside of you. It may be anxiety, but it is not fear. I want you to understand that you can still possess the promise if you do not allow your crazy thinking to dictate what comes out of your mouth. That is why the Bible instructs you to "*Keep your heart with all diligence, for out of it spring the issues of life*" (Proverbs 4:23). God also says: "*Death and life are in the power of the tongue...*" (Proverbs 18:21).

Fight the Faith Fight

Matthew chapter 8 gives an example of faith versus fear. It reads beginning at verse 23: *"Now when He got into a boat, His disciples followed Him. And suddenly a great tempest arose on the sea, so that the boat was covered with the waves. But He was asleep. Then His disciples came to Him and awoke Him, saying, 'Lord, save us! We are perishing!' But He said to them, 'Why are you fearful, O you of little faith?' "* (Matthew 8:23-26)

I want you to understand that Jesus was asleep. He was not conscious of what was happening around Him—He was asleep in a storm. He was no more conscious of what was going on in the earth realm than you are when you are asleep. He was not picking something up in the Spirit while He was asleep. He ministered as a man anointed with the Spirit of God.

Jesus was not conscious of where they were either emotionally or spiritually. But when they woke Him up, they said to Him, *"Lord, save us! We are perishing!"* That is all Jesus heard, and Jesus looked at them and said, *"Why are you fearful...?"* In essence, Jesus said that what they just said to Him was a statement of fear. He was not sensing fear when He was asleep. *Jesus knew they were afraid because of what they said.*

His disciples were fishermen. They lived by the sea and were accustomed to waves and motion. They knew that anyone who went out into a storm like the one they were in was in jeopardy of death. They had seen that kind of storm before, and their experience told them that kind of storm could kill them. They knew that if the storm did not stop, they were going to die. They believed their circumstance— that the storm would kill them.

When they woke Jesus for Him to address their situation, He responded with, *"Why are you fearful, O you of little*

71

faith?" In other words, you can choose which one to use. Your faith is little because you have not been exercising it; and if you would exercise it, then you would not have to wake God up for everything!

That is the difference between the child of God whose faith is growing and the child of God who has spent twenty years in church and still has little faith. One is exercising his faith and, therefore, his faith is growing. The other has little faith.

"It is not fear until it comes out of you."

Your mind may be telling you all manner of things in your current situation. Just because you are feeling anxiety about the move God is telling you to make does not mean that you are in fear. In the same way that your belief alone about something does not mean you are in faith, your belief alone in something negative does not mean you are in fear. It is not fear until it comes out of you. However, if you believe that you are in fear, then you will not walk in faith.

If you believe the wrong thing is fear, then you will believe that you have already lost what God has promised you because you know that fear does not produce anything for you. The problem is that you have become so fear-conscious that you have believed Satan and religion's definition of fear. Some of you are in faith and you do not even realize it.

Another example is in Mark 5:21-23. It reads:

Now when Jesus had crossed over again by boat to the other side, a great multitude gathered to Him; and He was by the sea. And behold, one of the rulers of the synagogue came, Jairus by name. And when he saw Him, he fell at His feet and begged Him earnestly, saying, 'My little daughter lies at the point of death. Come and lay Your hands on her, that she may be healed, and she will live.

This was Old Covenant. (The New Covenant was not in effect until after the Resurrection!) Jairus was speaking forward to the cross; but it was a statement of faith according to his covenant. I want you to see something here. Jairus made his statement of faith by saying, *"and she will live."* Jesus went with him *after* he made his statement of faith. In other words, when he spoke his faith, the power of God went with him because Jesus is the Living Word. So, the Word of God went to work—the Word started moving in his circumstance. Look at verse 24: *"So Jesus went with him, and a great multitude followed Him and thronged Him."*

At this point, Jesus was on His way to Jairus' house. The Scripture continues with, *"Now a certain woman had a flow of blood for twelve years, and had suffered many things from many physicians. She had spent all that she had and was no better, but rather grew worse"* (Mark 5:25-26).

You know the story—she heard of Jesus and she was healed when she touched His garment; then Jesus asked who it was that touched Him. Get it. She was hiding and the Bible declares that she told Him all that happened, which was how the writer got the information to record it. And Jesus responded with, *"Daughter, your faith has made you well. Go in peace, and be healed of your affliction"* (Mark 5:34). He did not say, "My power has made you well," but "Your faith has made you well." Jesus knew that His power had always been there, but it was not until someone's conviction or persuasion plus corresponding action pulled on His power that something happened. It was

73

not Jesus' anointing that healed her; it was her conviction or persuasion plus corresponding action.

Continuing in the Scripture, the writer again addresses Jairus' situation. The Bible records: "*While He was still speaking, some came from the ruler of the synagogue's house who said, 'Your daughter is dead. Why trouble the Teacher any further?' "* (Mark 5:35) Do not miss the point here. The Word of God was already moving toward Jairus' circumstance. So then, Jairus was literally walking with the Word, and while the Word was moving in his situation, a negative report came to him that told him not to trouble the Teacher any further.

The Bible says in verse 36, "*As soon as Jesus heard the word that was spoken, He said...'Do not be afraid, only believe.' "* He told Jairus not to be afraid. The King James translation says, "Do not fear." In other words, whatever you do, do not fear. Why would Jesus tell Jairus not to fear? It was because he was walking with Jesus. The Word was already moving toward his situation. The power of God was already directed toward his daughter because of his confession of faith.

I want you to understand something that is very important. If you have children, then you know that hearing a report that your child has just died causes an emotional response within you. There will be some anxiety and sorrow, especially if you had been on your way to get them help. But, Jesus looked at Jairus and said, "Do not fear." If fear were an emotion, then Jesus would not have said that to him, because it is impossible to hear that your child is dead and not have an emotional reaction.

He was not telling Jairus not to have any emotion. He was telling him not to let his emotions change his confession. He said, "Wait a minute, Jairus. Do not say anything. If you speak what they just said, then I am not going to your house. I will not be able to go to your house. I am walking with you right now because of what you said, and if you change what you say, then I will not be able to walk with you." In other words, Jesus told Jairus, "You have the right to remain silent. Anything you say, can and will be used against you in the court of Heaven. You have already confessed your Word of faith, so do not say anything else!"

I am sure that Jairus must have done the same thing that most of us do. He said, "But, but, but…Jesus." And Jesus said, "Ssshhh! Do not respond to that. Be quiet and let Me [the Living Word] do this. Do not fear. I know you heard it because I heard it, but do not speak it. If you do not speak it, then it is not fear." The truth is that the Word was on its way to Jairus' house. The truth is that the Resurrection and the Life was on the way to his house. The fact of the matter is that Jairus said nothing for the rest of the walk.

Because he said nothing else, Jairus was still walking with his confession, which was, "If You come and lay Your hands on her, **she will live**." Jairus was walking in that Word. As a result, Jesus went and took Peter, James, and John with Him. He put the doubt out of the house and surrounded Himself with people of faith—with people who lived like He lived, said what He said, and spoke how He spoke. Jesus then reached out and took the girl by the hand saying, "*Talitha, cumi*" (Mark 5:41).

Jesus wanted Jairus to understand that if he were to speak the report that he heard, then he would have released fear into his situation instead of faith. It is a matter of what comes out of your mouth. The truth of the matter is that if you do not get the Word of God in your mouth, then you have no other choice but to speak your circumstance and God calls that fear. Fear or faith—it is your choice.

Chapter 5

Know How to Work Your Faith

Chapter 5

Know How to Work Your Faith

———————

What we are about to get into is a significant element of the walk of faith and living by faith. We have established, over previous chapters some powerful and incredible truths concerning faith: what it is, how you walk by it, what it really means, and what the Bible actually means when it talks about faith. Now we are going to discuss how faith comes.

The Bible says that *"without faith it is impossible to please Him"* (Hebrew 11:6). It also says *"the just shall live by faith"* (Romans 1:17). Therefore, in order to please God, you must have faith. In order to live, you have to have faith, and so, you need to know how it comes because faith is something that "comes." It is not something that you just have. In this chapter, we are going to qualify what is meant by faith. We will begin with Romans 10:17—a passage of Scripture that is very familiar to you by now: "*So then faith comes by hearing, and hearing by the word of God.*"

Let us stop right there. I want you to check your own Bible and make sure that what you just read was, indeed, Romans 10:17. I want you to read it again because this verse is going to change before your very eyes: "*So then faith comes by hearing, and hearing by the word of God.*"

Romans 10:17 is familiar, but I am convinced that most Christians do not really understand what this verse is saying. Remember what faith is. Remember what James 2:17 says: "*Thus also faith by itself, if it does not have works, is dead.*"

Most people think of faith as belief. So when the Bible says in Romans 10:7 that "*faith comes by hearing, and hearing by the word of God,*" most Christians think it means that "believing" comes by hearing. They think that faith *is* belief and belief *is* faith, but the Bible is clear that belief and faith are different things. You must know and understand how faith comes if you are going to exercise faith and stop allowing the devil to tell you that you do not have enough faith for what you are believing God to do.

You must develop your faith. It is not as if you are unable to get faith, but one of the things you have to understand is that you are never going to get more faith by asking God for it—that is not how faith comes. God is not going to give you more faith simply because you pray for it. You might say, "Bishop, how can you possibly say that?" Because God has told you and me in His Word how faith comes, and He has told us that faith is not a product of you asking for it and God giving it to you.

James 2:17 says, "*Thus also faith,*" or conviction or persuasion, without "*works,*" or corresponding action, is dead. So,

James is telling us by the inspiration of the Holy Spirit that conviction or persuasion, if it does not have corresponding action, is dead. Verses 18-19 continue:

> *But someone will say, "You have faith, and I have works." Show me your faith without your works, and I will show you my faith by my works. You believe that there is one God. You do well. Even the demons believe—and tremble!* (James 2:18-19)

In other words, devils believe! Okay, it is good that you believe, but understand that believing is not Bible Faith. He says, *"demons believe,"* but that doesn't make them change anything. They do not please God. The reason they do not please God is because their corresponding actions never line up with what they believe. Demons know Jesus is Lord, but they do not act in accordance with that knowledge. The Bible tells us that they know Jesus is Lord because it says *"As I live, says the Lord, every knee shall bow to Me, and every tongue shall confess to God"* (Romans 14:11).

People get healed because demons know that Jesus is Lord. People get set free from addictions when believers pray because demons know that Jesus is Lord. They just do not act upon that knowledge until somebody with more authority than they have comes and makes them obey. However, if you do not know that you have this authority, then you sit there and let them whip you and think, *Well, it must be God's will.* No! It is not God's will! It is because of your lack of will, your lack of knowledge, and your lack of information.

Let us look at one more verse where this concept is explained. Notice what He says in verse 26 of James chapter 2:

"For as the body without the spirit is dead, so faith without works is dead also." Now get what He is saying. Faith is likened to the body, which can do nothing without the spirit because your spirit is what gives life to your body. The body without the spirit is dead. It is inoperative. It takes a spirit to give animation, life, and physicality. It takes a spirit to cause the body to do anything. So, now notice what James says. He says that your belief (or your conviction or your persuasion **without corresponding action**) is dead. It will produce nothing.

Now that you understand this working definition of faith, let us look at Romans 10:17 again. A working definition means that any place where you see the word *faith* in the New Testament, you can insert that working definition and read it with clarity. So, in Romans 10:17 (KJV) where Paul says, *"So then, faith cometh by hearing and hearing by the word of God,"* we can insert the James 2:14 working definition—conviction or persuasion plus corresponding action. Therefore, with our working definition, Romans 10:17 reads: "So then conviction or persuasion **plus corresponding action** cometh by hearing, and hearing by the word of God." This is mind-blowing! This proves beyond a shadow of a doubt that your believing is not faith and your faith is not believing. Until your believing becomes faith, nothing is going to happen.

What this verse is telling you is that you will not act upon what you say you believe unless you are hearing what you say you believe. (Read that sentence again!) Now, you believe it before you act on this, but believing is not faith, and faith is not believing. Remember, it is never faith on the inside of you. On the inside of you, it is a conviction or a persuasion. On the inside of you, it is something you believe, but that is not faith. It is not faith until it has a corresponding action. So, it is not faith until it can be heard or seen. **Because of that, nobody else can ever give you faith.** Preachers cannot give you faith. Tapes cannot give you faith. Books cannot give you faith. A preacher can help you to believe or to become persuaded and convinced, but that is not faith.

I know I am being very methodical, but I must make sure you understand this completely. Once you get this, you will know how to get faith for whatever you are believing for. You will stop waiting for angels to drop by in the night with little "faith packages." You will stop waiting to get faith until you can get to church, the next miracle meeting, the next crusade, or the next conference. You will start getting faith the way you are suppose to get it—by yourself through the authority that Jesus has given you as one who is blood-bought and full of His Spirit, with access to His Word!

Now look at Romans 10:14. It reads: *"How then shall they call on Him in whom they have not believed? And how shall they believe in Him of whom they have not heard? And how shall they hear without a preacher?"* Now, get this! He says, *"How shall they believe in Him whom they have not **heard**?"* This means that you will not believe anything until you have heard it.

But faith is not believing. Now get it, you cannot believe until you have heard, but the Bible says *"you do believe what you have heard."* See, hearing causes me to believe. Notice the tense of what he says.

You can believe what you **have heard**, but believing only becomes faith by what you **are hearing**. I am going to say it one more time. Get it! You can believe what you have heard—past tense. In other words, I have heard it and I believe it, but that is not faith. **You can believe what you have heard, but believing becomes faith only by what you are hearing—***present* **tense.** Notice what he says, *"So then faith cometh."* Faith is not present when you get the Word; it cometh. What happened is when you heard, you believed. Faith, however, does not come until you keep hearing what it is you have heard that you believed. That is why I am telling you that no other individual can give you faith. I submit to you that when the Bible says *"faith cometh by hearing,"* it tells us that the only way faith is going to come is if you start speaking the Word to you, not if somebody else speaks the Word to you. This is the only way for you to gain faith because nobody else is going to be around you all the time speaking the Word to you.

We have become too dependent on preachers. We want them to stay around us all the time and preach the Word or give us a word. God has given *you* thousands of "words" in the Bible, so how is it that you have no faith? Let me break it down to you.

The preacher preaches something to you from the Word of God, and you see it in the Word. When the preacher preaches it to you, you believe it because you can see it in your own Bible. You also believe it because the Holy Spirit witnesses to your re-created, born-again spirit that it is truth. At that point, you believe what has been preached to you, but you do not have faith for what has been preached to you because **faith cometh.**

Look at verse 14 again: *"How then shall they call on Him in whom they have not believed? And how shall they believe in Him of whom they have not heard?"* This tells me that the objective of my believing is so I can say something, not just so I can be convinced. He says, *"How shall they call?"* The objective of getting the Word is so you can "**call**." The objective of getting persuaded, or the objective of believing something, is so that you can **call**. It is not so that you can walk around saying, "I believe, I believe, I believe." There are a lot of people who believe in prosperity; they believe the Bible says they should prosper. However, they do not have faith for it because they have not been **calling** Jehovah Jireh—the Lord my Provider. They have not been declaring, "My need is met." They believe it but do not have faith for it because they have not been saying it.

The objective of my getting convinced or persuaded is so I can say something. So when the preacher tells me and gives evidence from the Word that Jesus is Jehovah Rapha—the Lord my Healer—the objective is to persuade me and cause me to believe it. Then I can use that belief and persuasion to begin telling myself that the Lord is my healer and I am healed. Once I do this, I have faith—it is up to me.

*It is not faith when **I** say it to you; it is faith when **you** say it to you.* When I say it to you, it is only assistance in getting you to believe. I am trying to make a believer out of you. God has called you a believer, so I use my faith, my energy, my sweat, and my prayer to make sure that you are what He says you are. The believing is to get you to call, and you can believe what you have heard, *but you can only have faith when what you have heard becomes what you are hearing.*

Now let's look at Hebrews 4:1-2:

Therefore, since a promise remains of entering His rest, let us fear lest any of you seem to have come short of it. For *indeed the gospel was preached to us as well as to them; but the word which they heard did not profit them, not being **mixed with faith** in those who heard it.*

So they did hear it, but even though they did hear it, it never became faith. They heard, and you can believe what you have heard—past tense—but they did not mix faithwith it!

For instance, you can go to the store and buy instant cake mix—instant means immediate cake. You can go and get instant cake mix, but you also know you cannot take that cake mix home, open the package, pour it down your throat, and have cake. It will not look or taste like cake. In this case you understand that "instant" does not mean that it is cake in the form in which you bought it. You understand that it will not be cake until you take it home and mix it with other ingredients. The store does not give you those ingredients when you buy the cake. The store expects that if you really want to eat this cake, you will add the necessary ingredients to what you have in order for you to make it.

Likewise, the promises of God are instant; they are already done! God has said, *"For all the promises of God in Him are Yes, and in Him Amen, to the glory of God..."* (2 Corinthians 1:20). They are instant. However, in order to eat of the good of the land, you have to take the Word home and mix it! No one can mix it for you. *You* have to mix it. God is not going to mix it.

Many have thought that faith comes with the Word. No, it does not! If faith came with the Word *heard*, then they would have had faith when they heard the Word. We have read in the Bible, *"For indeed the gospel was preached to us as well as to them; but the word which they heard did not profit them, not being mixed with faith in those who heard it"* (Hebrews 4:2). So, if the Word alone brought faith, they would not have had to mix it.

They heard the Good News just like you and I are weekly hearing Good News. But the Word that they heard (past tense) did not profit them, because it was a Word that was heard, not a Word that they were hearing, and only a hearing Word will profit you. A heard Word will not heal you, only a hearing Word. *A heard Word will not deliver you, only a hearing Word.* Hearing is present tense. Only a hearing Word will profit you. If I am believing God for something, my job is to take the Word *heard* and make it a Word I am *hearing.* My job is to take a *heard* Word and mix it into a *hearing* Word. I like what Dr. Fredrick K.C. Price says… "The mixing bowl is your mouth, and the beater blade is your tongue." The question is, Are you in the mix?

No one else, including God, is responsible for the level of faith that I am walking in. I know this may be a little frightening at first because it takes us out of a false dependence on God, but once you get it, you get absolutely delivered. In the Old Covenant, God *gave them* a Word. In the New Covenant, He has *already given us* His Word. So, it is not like God is going to appear to you now and tell you what to say because He has already appeared in the person of His Son.

If you are waiting on a word, God has already given you all the *words* you need to *start faith* in you concerning anything He said to you. It is called the Bible. You are waiting on a word, and He is saying, "I have already given you all the words." You need to get started. You have been leaning on the Lord, and you are leaning so far now that you are about to fall. You have been leaning on the Lord, and you have not understood that leaning on the Lord is not going to get you into what He has promised you. It is a little uncomfortable at first, but once you get it, it is absolutely liberating because now you understand that nobody can keep your faith level from going through the roof except you—not even the devil! This does not take any importance from God, for He says Himself that we are to look to His Word. Second Timothy 2:15 (KJV) says: "*Study to show thyself approved unto God, a workman that needeth not to be ashamed, rightly dividing the word of truth.*"

If all I do is read the Bible, then I will not show myself approved as a workman of it. However, if I study, I will manifest the fact that I have God's approval because I am working the Word. That is what a workman does, and I will not need to be ashamed. Sad to say, most Christians are ashamed. They say they serve God, but they cannot pay their bills. They say they serve God, but their family is in crisis 24/7 (24 hours/7 days a week). Most Christians do not have any evidence that they are any different than the people they go to work with. They go to church and they read their Bible, but they do not study to show themselves approved. They do not work the Word. The Word is not just to be read; it is to be worked!

Rightly dividing the Word of truth is not just an ability to articulate it and interpret it. Rightly dividing the Word of truth is knowing what is useful for what. Some of us need to understand that this has been given to us. If I am believing God for prosperity, I need to study what the Bible has to say about prosperity. If I am believing God for my health, I need to study what the Bible has to say about healing. If I have low self-esteem, I need to study what the Bible has to say about righteousness.

Beyond Personal Power

I have one more example for you. The woman with the issue of blood was not healed by the Word she heard. Look at Mark 5:25-34:

> *Now a certain woman had a flow of blood for twelve years, and had suffered many things from many physicians. She had spent all that she had and was no better, but rather grew worse. When she heard about Jesus, she came behind **Him** in the crowd and touched His garment. For she said, "If only I may touch His clothes, I shall be made well." Immediately the fountain of her blood was dried up, and she felt in her body that she was healed of the affliction. And Jesus, immediately knowing in Himself that power had gone out of Him, turned around in the crowd and said, "Who touched My clothes?" But His disciples said to Him, "You see the multitude thronging You, and You say, 'Who touched Me?'" And He looked around to see her who had done this thing. But the woman, fearing and trembling, knowing what had happened to her, came and fell down before Him and told Him the whole truth. And He said to her, "Daughter, your faith has made you well"* (emphasis added).

Verse 28 says, *"For she said…"* and if you study this further, you find that it is a continuous action. Watch this! After Jesus feels her touch the hem of His garment, He says to her, *"Your faith has made you well."* Her conviction or persuasion plus her corresponding action is what made her well, not anything Jesus said or did. It was her faith!

Now, let me break this down for you. What she said was not what she heard because Jesus was not preaching, nor was anybody else preaching; nor had anybody else done what she did. She *heard* that this Man was healing people. She *heard* that He was multiplying loaves and fishes. She *heard* that He was healing blind eyes. She *heard* that lame people were walking. She *heard* that dead people were being raised up. But she did not hear that people were touching His garment and being made well. Nobody was preaching, "Touch His garment and you will be healed." Nobody was preaching that! So, it was not the word she *heard* about Jesus that gave her the faith. The Word that she *was hearing* **convinced** her that He could heal.

"Your faith has made you well."

If you know anything about the Old Covenant, you know that what she was hearing convinced her that He was a priest and a prophet because the Old Covenant said that if you were a priest or a prophet, you would be anointed with oil. The oil, however, was not to touch His flesh (see Exodus 30:31-32), but that oil would be in His garment. Based on that covenant she knew that if He was a priest, there had to be oil in that garment.

Remember that this is Old Covenant; therefore, the price for her healing had not yet been paid in full. That price would be paid at the cross upon which Jesus had not yet been hung. All the miracles of Jesus' earthly ministry that are written in the New Testament are really under the Old Covenant. The New Covenant or Testament actually began with the Book of Acts, not with Matthew. Until the Book of Acts, the price of redemption was not paid in full. Your Bible tells you that for a testament to be enforced, it first requires the death of the testator, who is Jesus Christ (see Hebrew 9:17). So, again, this is Old Covenant. Jesus said Himself, *"Do not think that I came to destroy the Law or the Prophets. I did not come to destroy but to fulfill"* (Matthew 5:17). This means everything He did in His earthly ministry was a fulfillment of the Old Covenant and, when He died, the New Covenant began. So, this woman was in the Old Covenant. The price of redemption had not been paid in full. Therefore, in this case, power went out of Him.

Under the New Covenant, all the power that is coming out of Him has already come out. The power to change your situation is not going to come out of Him now—it is already out of Him. When He sent the Holy Ghost, that was the power coming out of Him. I want you to understand, God has already released His power to us. All the power that is coming out of Him is out of Him, and it is already in the earth. His name is Holy Spirit. *He* is the power of God. We are not waiting for power to be released now; we are waiting for Christians to connect, and the way you connect now is by your faith.

If it was His power being released that caused your prosperity, you would be prospered now! The Bible is telling you that the power went out of Him. Jesus told the woman that His power did not heal her. It was her faith. In other words, it is really not what He said that got her healed because she had not even heard Him. It was actually what *she said about what she heard*. That is why what you hear is so important. You are going to say what you hear.

She started saying, *"If only I may touch His clothes, I shall be made well"* (Mark 5:28). But she hadn't heard that about Jesus. *That is what she heard herself say.* She heard herself keep saying it. Faith did not come by what somebody else had told her about Jesus; faith came by what she was telling herself!

She sat in that rocking chair, day after day, bleeding and hemorrhaging, hearing He could heal, and she said, *"If I can just touch the hem of His garment, I will be made well—if I could just touch the hem of His garment.*" She said it so much that she finally decided that she was not going to sit down one more day. **She decided to get up and act out her faith**.

The faith came by what she was saying, not by what was preached. What was preached caused her to start "calling." And when she started mixing her faith, it started coming; and the more she said it, the more she saw it; and the more she saw it, the more her faith grew: "I have to get out of this chair; I have to get out of this chair. He can heal, but nothing is going to happen unless I get out of this chair. I know the law says because I am a hemorrhaging woman, I do not have any right to be in any assembly [because a woman with an issue of blood was ceremonially unclean and could not go amongst the congregation]. But if I can just touch the hem of His garment, I will be made whole." And she touched and was made whole because you will have what you say.

Child of God, you hear yourself speak more than anyone else. It is not what I tell you that is going to determine your outcome; it is what you tell yourself based on the Word of God. What I tell you is only so you can believe. Now someone will say, "Yes, but, Bishop, what about that Scripture that says that God has dealt to every man the measure of faith"? Read it—*the measure* of faith. It does not say, *a* measure; it says, *the* measure. A measure means that God arbitrarily decides who gets what—"I am going to give you more faith than I am going to give her because I like you better." But the Bible does not say that "God has given to man *a* measure of faith"; it says that "*...God hath dealt to every man the measure of faith*" (Romans 12:3 KJV). I was reading that one day and I asked God, "Lord, help me understand this."

Beyond Personal Power

He said, "I said, *the* measure." Measure is a standard of rule. Measure is the means of determining how much. So when God says, "*I have dealt to every man the measure of faith,*" **He is saying that He has given each of us the standard by which we can measure whether we are in faith or not!** He has given each of us the ruler by which we can determine whether we are in faith or not. See, a ruler is how I determine how long something is. A measuring stick is called a ruler because it determines length. God is saying, "I have given you the ruler, so you can determine whether you actually have any faith or not; your Bible is the ruler." If what you have is what the Bible says, then it is faith.

When you are measuring carpet, if your ruler says it is twelve feet long, you cannot claim it is fifteen feet long. The ruler tells you how long it is. You cannot value it as you would a fifteen-foot piece of carpet and expect someone to buy it. The ruler said it is twelve feet long…period. In a similar fashion, God has given you the ruler of faith, but we call what we are doing faith, even though it is not working and nothing is manifested. You may have been doing things one way for years with no results, but you still say, "Oh well, I have faith. " But God says, "Measure it against the ruler."

Chapter 6

Pray the Prayer of Faith

Chapter 6

Pray the Prayer of Faith

——•——

The Spirit of the Lord spoke in my spirit and literally said, "Son, I want you to teach in this area, because this is a vital subject for My people to understand in their walk of faith. This area is where many of My people miss it: praying the prayer of faith." He said, "Bring understanding to My people so that they can get their saying and their praying consistent."

> *Is anyone among you suffering? Let him pray. Is anyone cheerful? Let him sing psalms. Is anyone among you sick? Let him call for the elders of the church, and let them pray over him, anointing him with oil in the name of the Lord. And the prayer of faith will save the sick, and the Lord will raise him up. And if he has committed sins, he will be forgiven* (James 5:13-15).

Pray the Prayer of Faith

James tells us that the prayer of faith will save the sick. Notice, he does not just say that "prayer will save the sick"; he says, "the prayer of faith will save." So it is not just prayer, but it is the **prayer of faith**. This word *save* here is the word *sozo* in Greek, which actually means "to set free, deliver or rescue." And because we are talking about an eternal law, this principle will work for anything. The prayer of faith *will* deliver from sickness or poverty or anything else and will save you and your household.

Our working definition of faith is found in James chapter 2, and anywhere you see the word *faith* in the New Covenant, insert that biblical working definition to get clarity in what the Word is telling you. Now, when the Bible speaks of faith, it is talking about a conviction or persuasion—in other words, believing plus corresponding action. In Second Corinthians 4:13, Paul says: *"And since we have the same spirit of faith, according to what is written, 'I believed and therefore I spoke,' we also believe and therefore speak."* There, the word *spirit* does not refer to necessarily an entity or a deity, but the word actually means *vital principle and mental disposition*. (I know we've be through this already, but it is vital that we go through it at each step!)

Faith has a vital principle, which is faith "speaks what it believes." The man or woman who is walking or living by faith sees things a certain way. According to Romans 10:8, the mental disposition of faith is that *"the word is near you, in your mouth and in your heart…."* That *is* the word of faith. The mental disposition of faith *is* that **it *is* always present tense, or that faith *is* always *is*.** A statement of faith is stated in the present tense, not in the past or the future tense, but faith says, "*It is.*"

So when James tells us that the prayer of faith will save the sick and deliver, he is telling us about a certain way of praying that will bring deliverance. The word *pray* in James chapter 5 is the Greek word *proseuchomai*, which is translated "pray" in Matthew 6 and Luke 11, where Jesus responds to His disciples when they say, "Master, teach us to pray." The Greek word *proseuchomai* actually means to "make a vow or a declaration in the direction of God." Understanding that is what prayer means, expands your definition of prayer. Based on what this word really means, prayer is not just asking God for something.

Religion has taught us that I am praying when I ask, or if I get in a certain posture, or if it sounds a certain way. Yet, when you understand the true biblical definition of prayer, you can begin to fulfill the command given in the Scripture to pray without ceasing. That does not mean that I have to be somewhere shut off from people in a closed room all my life, so spiritually-minded that I am no earthly good. James is saying that the vow or declaration made in the direction of God, prayer that speaks what it believes in the present tense of faith, *will* deliver!

> *So Jesus answered and said to them, "Have faith in God. For assuredly, I say to you, whoever says to this mountain, 'Be removed and be cast into the sea,' and does not doubt in his heart, but believes that those things he says will be done, he will have whatever he says. Therefore I say to you, whatever things you ask when you pray, believe that you receive them, and you will have them"* (Mark 11:22-24).

96

The word *therefore* in verse 24 is key because that word ties the previous statement to the statement that follows. What is Jesus saying here? That you are going to have whatever you say. "That is why I say to you, what things so ever you desire when you pray, believe you receive, because you are going to have whatever you *say*." Therefore, when you pray, believe you receive, because if you believe you receive when you pray, *then* after you have prayed, you will say, "I have." If you do not believe you receive when you pray, then you will say, "I am going to" or "God is going to." If you say, "God is going to," you will have a God who is always "going to" and never seems to manifest anything *now*!

Many Christians die in the wilderness of unbelief because they have a God who is always going to do something but never seems to manifest anything. Why? Because they are always saying, "He is going to" and "the Lord is about to work it out." So you have a God who is always about to work things out—He never finishes anything. You have a God who is always "about to bless," so you are always on the verge of a miracle and never get one. But when you begin to believe you receive, you cease to have a God who is going to do something, and you now have a God who has done; and because He has done, you do have. So believe you receive when you pray, *not after.*

The New King James version says, *"Whatever things you ask"*; the King James says, *"What things soever ye desire."* As believers, our desire should be the will of God. Now, sometimes my desires and your desires are not in line with God's desires, and that is why we have to wait until we know that our desires have lined up. How do you get there? By exercising faith and saying, "My desires are God's desires."

As believers, we are to desire the Word of God, or the will of God. The will of God *is* the Word of God. That is why it is called "a testament," because it is the last will and testament of Yahweh for His people. So understand that if you constantly ignore going to church, what you are doing is willingly deciding to be absent from the reading of your will. If someone dies and leaves you an inheritance and you are not present at the reading of the will, you cannot contest whether what you are told is true or false because you do not have the information. So you better be there (a Bible-preaching and teaching church) when the will is read!

We could say it this way: When you pray the Word of God (which is the will of God, which should be what you desire) and believe that you receive the Word of God (which is the will of God, which should be what you desire), you shall *have* the Word of God (which is the will of God, which should be what you desire). "Therefore, I say to you, when you pray My word, which is My will, which should be what you desire, make sure that you pray My word in the language or tense of believing you receive, and you will have." Therefore, if God's promise says, "He will," then my prayer of faith back to Him is not "He will," but "He has" or "It is done!" So God says, "I will supply all your needs," and I say, "My need **is** supplied."

I ask God to meet my need, and from the moment I ask Him, when I pray, as I am still praying, I say, "Now, Father, I thank You that I receive this need met." Therefore, right now, while I am still praying, I declare that this need is met in Jesus' name, and I praise, worship and glorify Him that this is done. Amen! Now, the next time I go to pray, that need is something that I believe I have already received. So, I am not asking for that again; because if I ask for that again, then I am testifying to God that I did not believe I received when I prayed yesterday. Because if I believe I received when I prayed yesterday, then I am not going to ask for it again today. Thus, Jesus is saying, *"You must get your praying in line with your saying, and your saying in line with your praying, because you will not get what you pray; you will get what you say."*

If you are saying one thing and praying another, you are in contradiction. Christians have to understand that God is not a legalist, but Satan is. He is the accuser of the brethren. God is a God of integrity, and He bases everything that He does on His Word. Your God, Jehovah, is the God who said, *"The just shall live by faith."* God is not going to break His Word for *you*. Because if He breaks His Word, then He loses His integrity with the rest of us.

If God simply blessed His people who have no faith, after having said, *"The just shall live by faith,"* then Satan could accuse God, saying, "You are a liar—You said they had to live by faith, but You are blessing them while they are not living by faith. Their words are contradictory to everything You say, and You are blessing them." God will not be put in a position where He is accused by Satan of breaking His Word. Therefore He says, "To My people, My justified, My redeemed, you have to learn to live by faith." This answers the question a lot of Christians have as to why it was that before getting saved, God answered a couple of their prayers even though they knew nothing about faith.

Beyond Personal Power

Now that they are saved, they ask, "Why is that I have to jump through the faith hoop and make sure my confession is right and in the right tense?" Before you were born again, the statement made by Jehovah, *"The just shall live by faith"* did not apply to you. You were not one of the just. So, God could answer your prayer without breaking His Word, because you did not pray in faith—you just asked. You were poor, desperate, and pitiful; and God said, "Understand this is mercy. You do not have any right to this, and this is not going to work for you all the time; but I want you to know I am out here. I want you to know I hear you and that there really is a God." So, He answered you to draw you, so you could believe and become *one of the just.* Now that you have become one of the just, He says, "Now, if you want this to work, you have got to learn how to live by faith, because now 'the just shall live by faith' is the Word that I am bound to concerning you."

The issue of getting one's saying and praying in agreement is where many Christians have missed it. Many will confess God's Word and decree that their need is met. But when they go to prayer, they ask God for the very thing they have been saying is done. They say, "Lord, I thank You that by Your stripes I am healed," and later they pray, "God, my back is still aching, and I am asking You in the name of Jesus to heal me." But you just said that you were healed, and now you are asking Him to do something you said you had. It is inconsistent and will not work!

There are also people who have learned how to pray, "God, I thank You," but when they get out of the prayer closet and someone asks them, "How is it going?" they say, "The

Lord will make a way somehow." But wait, you just said in prayer, "Thank You," and now He is about to come through? James understood this principle:

> *If any of you lacks wisdom, let him ask of God, who gives to all liberally and without reproach, and it will be given to him. But let him ask in faith, with no doubting, for he who doubts is like a wave of the sea driven and tossed by the wind. For let not that man suppose that he will receive anything from the Lord* (James 1:5-7).

Understand that the point of this passage is not wisdom, **but lack**! The principle applies to whatever! Not **what** you lack, but *that* you lack. He said, "If any of you lacks wisdom (or anything else), ask God for it." But here is the caveat— you must ask in faith. Now again, faith is conviction or persuasion plus corresponding action. The spirit of faith speaks what it believes in the present tense. He is saying, "If any of you lacks anything, ask God for it. But remember, when you ask, you have got to be speaking what you believe in the present tense." If you do not do that, do not think you will get anything from the Lord. If you do not get this discipline down you will be double-minded, or the Greek word *dipsukos*, which means two minds or spiritually schizophrenic. In other words, whichever way the wind is blowing that day, that is what you will say. So, if we get up today and it looks good, we say, "Oh, it's happening"; and tomorrow, if we get up and it does not look good, we say, "Oh, I do not know what is going on."

Let him ask in the spirit of faith. When he asks let him say, "Now, Lord, I believe I receive it, and I thank You that I have it. Therefore, I praise You that I have it" with no doubting. Remember, doubting has nothing to do with what you are feeling, *but only with what you say.* If it does not come out of your mouth, it is not doubt. If it does not come out of your mouth, it is not fear. You can feel like you are about to sink and never rise again, but if you do not let it come out of your mouth, it is not doubt. It is only faith when you speak it; likewise, it is only doubt when you speak it.

> *Elijah was a man with a nature like ours, and he prayed earnestly that it would not rain; and it did not rain on the land for three years and six months. And he prayed again, and the heaven gave rain, and the earth produced its fruit* (James 5:17-18).

The Bible says, "Elijah prayed that it would not rain" and he prayed again that it would rain, and it did. It also says that, He was a man of like passions or like nature with us. That is important because James is telling us to stop deifying Old Testament saints. They were men just like us, subject to the same ups-and-downs as you and I have; and as a matter of fact, they did not have a covenant as good as ours. The Bible says that you and I have a better covenant, based on better promises (see Hebrew 8:6). James says, "Look, Elijah was a man just like you and me. He was subject to his emotions and to other people's opinions. But he prayed that it would not rain, and it did not; and he prayed again, that it would rain, and it did." When the Bible says that Elijah prayed, it means just what it says—"Elijah prayed." The Bible supports everything it says, but nowhere in the Scripture do you see Elijah do what many people call prayer. But if what he did do is what the Bible calls prayer, then let's look at what Elijah did twice and gain knowledge by example of what the prayer of faith is!

And Elijah the Tishbite, of the inhabitants of Gilead, said to Ahab, "As the Lord God of Israel lives, before whom I stand, there shall not be dew nor rain these years, except at my word." Then the word of the Lord came to him, saying, "Get away from here and turn eastward, and hide by the Brook Cherith, which flows into the Jordan."…And it happened after a while that the brook dried up, because there had been no rain in the land (1 Kings 17:1-3,7).

The Bible says that Elijah prayed earnestly that it would not rain, and yet we do not see him with his eyes closed, rolling on the floor, asking God, "Oh God, shut up the heaven, Lord." No. He went to Ahab, who was king, and said, "My God is alive, and while I was in His presence, He told me it is not going to rain. So, Ahab, 'as the Lord God lives before whom I stand, there shall not be dew nor rain these years, until I say so.' And I am not going to say so until I hear God say so. I am only going to say what I hear Him say." And the Bible says, when Elijah did that, he prayed. The Bible calls *that* the prayer of faith. Now look at the second example.

And it came to pass after many days that the word of the Lord came to Elijah, in the third year, saying, "Go, present yourself to Ahab, and I will send rain on the earth."…Then Eljiah said to Ahab, "Go up, eat and drink; for there is the sound of abundance of rain." So Ahab went up to eat and drink. And Elijah went up to the top of Carmel; then he bowed down on the ground, and put his face between his knees, and said to his servant, "Go up now, look toward the

*sea." So he went up and looked, and said, "There is noth-
ing." And seven times he said, "Go again." Then it came to
pass the seventh time, that he said, "There is a cloud, as
small as a man's hand, rising out of the sea!" So he said,
"Go up, say to Ahab, 'Prepare your chariot, and go down
before the rain stops you.' " Now it happened in the mean-
time that the sky became black with clouds and wind, and
there was a heavy rain. So Ahab rode away and went to
Jezreel* (1 Kings 18:1,41-45).

God said, "I **will**," (1 Kings 18:1) but Elijah did not say,
"God is about to send rain." Elijah said, "There **is** the sound of
the abundance of rain" (1 Kings 18:41) and the Bible calls this
the prayer of faith. God says, "I **will** heal you," and the prayer
of faith is "I **am** healed." God says, "I will provide for you,"
and "My need is met; I am provided for in everything" is the
prayer of faith. *"So Ahab went up to eat and drink. And Elijah
went up to the top of Carmel; then he bowed down on the ground,
and put his face between his knees"* (1 Kings 18:42).

He had prayed the prayer of faith, then went up and put
his face between his knees. (Now, this is not an example for
you to sit in your house and say, "The Lord is making a way;
the Lord is working it out; I just believe.") Elijah had prayed
the prayer of faith. And when he had said in the present tense
what God had said, he got into the birthing position. For the
New Testament saint, the birthing position is revealed in
Philippians 4:6: *"Be anxious for nothing, but in everything by
prayer and supplication, with thanksgiving, let your requests be
made known to God."*

The birthing position is thanksgiving! The translation of
"thanksgiving" is grateful language. Notice, grateful language

is the birthing position—after you have prayed the prayer of faith, after you have said what God has said in the present tense. *"And said to his servant, 'Go up now, look toward the sea.' So he went up and looked, and said, 'There is nothing.' And seven times he said, 'Go again'"* (1 Kings 18:43). The servant here is "your feelings," "situation," and "experience." You have prayed the prayer of faith, declared what God said in the present tense and now you are in the birthing position: "Thank You, I believe I receive."

"Grateful language is the birthing position."

↲ The servant is a type of your feelings and it says, "I do not see anything." You are standing on the Word, believing the Word, and declaring the Word, saying "Thank You"; and your feelings say, "I do not see anything." Elijah said, "Go again," and the Bible says, "He did it seven times." Seven is the number of completion or maturity. In other words, Elijah stayed completely in the birthing position. He stayed completely in faith. He did not let the opinion of his feelings or circumstance get him out of position. He did not even respond when the servant said, "I do not see anything"; he just said, "Go again. Because I said it and God said it, I believe it—go again."

> *Then it came to pass the seventh time, that he said, "There is a cloud, as small as a man's hand, rising out of the sea!" So he said, "Go up, say to Ahab, 'Prepare your chariot, and go down before the rain stops you' "* (1 Kings 18:44).

There had not been any rain. All he saw was a cloud the size of a man's hand: This is the knowing that comes in the spirit before the manifestation, if you do not move out of the position. Not one drop of rain had come yet, so what is this? This is the preparation that comes if you believe you receive.

"God exists outside of time. Time is a creation of God."

Do you believe your need is met? Prepare! Some of you need to go to the house, write out the checks—do not mail them yet, but write them out. You believe all your bills are paid; you believe that God has met your need; you believe at the end of the month you are not going to lack. Go write out the checks, print the address on the envelope, get the stamp, lick it, and keep it on the table. Stop hesitating and prepare! This is not a trick—it is a walk of faith. It is not Bible roulette—you do not rub the Bible and wish! The prayer of faith will heal your body, will deliver your children, and will change your situation!

Faith Is a Timeless Creation

We must understand that God Almighty exists outside of time. Time came out of Him; time is a creation of God. It is literally a marker for the mortality of man and a way for us to number our days. The psalmist said, *"So teach us to number our days, that we may gain a heart of wisdom"* (Psalm 90:12). Teach me to understand that I have only got a certain amount of time to do what I have to do; therefore, I cannot afford to waste my time.

But God does not live in time. God lives outside of time, and because God lives outside of time, the only time God has is now. God has no past; He is eternal. Therefore, He does not hear what you said in your past, because He does not have one. So, when you speak, the only time God can hear you is now, because all He has is now. Therefore, if you are saying, "He will," from God's viewpoint, you are contradicting His *"is-ness"* because He has no future either. You cannot pray in the past or the future, so every time you pray, it is now; *it is*! That is why Jesus said in Mark 11:23, *"...whoever says to this mountain, 'Be removed and be cast into the sea,' and does not doubt in his heart, but believes that those things he says will be done, he will have whatever he says."*

Understand this revelation—the Gospels of Matthew, Mark, Luke, and John are not the beginning of the New Covenant; they are the fulfillment of the Old. The New Testament does not start with Matthew; the New Testament starts with Acts, because the New Covenant was not enforced until the death, burial, and resurrection of Jesus. When the death, burial, and resurrection occurred, then the New Covenant began. The last supper is called "last" because it is the last supper of the Old Covenant—it was the last Passover meal. It was not the last meal Jesus had with His disciples. He had fish and bread on the beach a few days after the resurrection (see John 21:9-12).

Every miracle that Jesus performed was under the Old Covenant, where the price for the things being requested had not been paid in full. It was like going to pick up something you had put on layaway but had not paid the balance for. Under the Old Covenant, people were coming to pick up things that had not been fully paid for. They had to come and say, "Lord, if You will speak." In Matthew 8:8, the centurion said, *"Lord...only speak a word, and my servant **will** be healed"* (emphasis added). They spoke in the future because they were dealing with a covenant not paid for. That was Old Covenant. But because what we have received is a "New Covenant," we must take what we see in the Old Covenant (as people approach Jesus) and apply it to our New Covenant.

"Examine yourselves as to whether you are in the faith. Test yourselves. Do you not know yourselves, that Jesus Christ is in you?—unless indeed you are disqualified. But I trust that you will know that we are not disqualified" (2 Corinthians 13:5-6). This is one of the Scriptures that God led me to when He spoke to me about taking the "Faith Exam." He said, "You need to check yourself out and make sure you are in faith." You need to make sure you know what faith is and make sure you are in it; without faith, you cannot please God, and without faith you are not going to have the God-Kind of life.

In other words, if you are redeemed, you are not disqualified. But Paul says, "Understand that your examination of yourself—to see whether you are in the faith or not—must take into account that Christ is now in you." You have got to take the New Testament exam, not the Old Covenant exam. If you take the exam with the information of the Old Covenant only, you will fail. Examine yourself to see whether you are in the faith; and as you are examining yourself, understand that your examination is based on the fact that Christ is in you. That means that now, in this covenant, you are not alone when you come to God to ask.

When I read the New Testament and the miracles of Jesus, I cannot adopt the dependent mentality of the Old Covenant. I cannot be the one who asks for something and then waits for God to speak. When we ask and then wait for God to speak, He says, "Wait a minute, do you not know for yourself that Christ is in you?" *So, the Person that you are waiting on to speak to your situation is in you!* The Lord has already said everything He's going to say, and He is in you.

I cannot examine my faith based on a second-dimension revelation. The revelation I have of Matthew, Mark, Luke and John is second-dimension—it is Old Covenant. I am in the New Covenant—I am now in the same spiritual class as Jesus. I am in the same spiritual class as the Jesus who did the speaking. (Most Christians miss this!) When Jesus worked that great miracle, people said, "What manner of man is this?" We miss the point that this is the manner of man that we are supposed to be.

So, I must be the one who prays, "Father, in the name of Jesus, based on the authority of Your Word, I am asking You to heal my body. For You said that Jesus was wounded for my transgressions and bruised for my iniquities. The chastisement of my peace was laid upon Him, and by His stripes I am healed. And so, right now, I believe that I receive my healing. I will not ask for this again, because I believe I receive when I pray. And so, right now, in the name of Jesus, I thank You for my healing."

Then, after I get up off my knees, I must assume the other position and say, "Now, devil, in the name of Jesus, I know this pain is still in my body, but you know and I know, I am healed." I am now speaking the Word. I must take the position of the one who comes and the one who speaks to the situation!

109

Beyond Personal Power

"Father, in the name of Jesus, I thank You that Your Word declares that You will supply all my needs. You know that I need $5,000 this month to meet my obligations, so I am asking You for the money, and in the name of Jesus, I believe, right now, I receive it." When I get up off my knees, I must take the other position and say, "My need is met." Because Christ is in you, He cannot speak into your situation if you are not talking. In Second Corinthians 13:5-6, the Holy Spirit tells us that when you examine yourself, make sure you examine yourself in light of the fact that the One you are coming to for answers is in you. He is saying, "I am here every time you are here. As a matter of fact, I go every place you go. You carry Me all the time."

Understand that you are qualified to stand in both positions. God made us joint heirs. I am now qualified to go to God for myself. I can go right into His presence, by the blood. I do not need anyone else to go in my place; I do not need a priest, a soothsayer, or a psychic friend. I can go to God myself and, when I am done, I can stand in my authority and tell the devil who I am, what I have and what belongs to me. This is why Jesus said, *All power is given unto Me in heaven and in earth* [because although I am going to Heaven, I am also going to be in you]" (Mathew 28:18 KJV).

The same power that is in you right now is going to be with you. It is going to be in the house with you, in the car with you, at work with you tomorrow. I am qualified and anointed to stand in both positions. It takes nothing from God when I stand in my authority. Someone says, "Where is God in all of this here?" He is up there saying, "That's My boy; go, man! Thank you for finally looking like My Son." Then, you lift your hands and thank Him that He is giving you this kind of power, because it all comes from Him. He gave it to you.

Beyond Personal Power

Chapter 7

Have Great Faith

Chapter 7

Have Great Faith

———⊶•⊷———

Before we move forward and examine what it means to have great faith, the Spirit of the Lord prompted me to say some things about the development of faith. First of all, great faith has nothing to do with size; rather, it has to do with intensity and application. Jesus said, *"If you had faith as a grain of mustard seed..."* (Luke 17:6 KJV). Read it for yourself. It has been misquoted as "If you had faith the *size* of." But that is not what it says. It says, "If you had faith *as*"; *"as"* is not only in reference to size, but also relates to what you do with a seed: You sow it. Jesus is saying, "If you have faith that you can and will continually sow, you can say to a mountain, 'Be removed,' and it will obey you." Someone may say, "Well, how do I sow my faith?" Mark 4:14 says, *"The sower sows the word"*—that is important. Regarding the development of faith, the Spirit of the Lord also told me to articulate that faith is like the fuel put in an automobile. It is what causes your spirit, soul, and body to move forward into the blessings and promises of God.

Now, what if you have more than one automobile? If you put fuel in your Cadillac all the time, but never fuel your Buick, you know that the Cadillac will run and the Buick will not. Just because you have fuel does not mean you are putting it in both cars. Faith is *like that*. Your faith has to be developed in various areas. You may have faith for healing and no faith for prosperity. Because you have faith does not mean it applies to everything; remember, faith is not believing and believing is not faith. If you are speaking God's Word concerning healing, but you are not putting the Word of prosperity in your mouth and heart, then you have faith for healing, but not prosperity; you will be healed but broke. You have to fuel every area of your life with the Word of God in order to be exercising faith in every area of your life.

"Faith is like fuel put in an automobile— it is what causes your spirit, soul, and body to move forward into the blessings and promises of God."

Looking at the foundation of great faith, there are only two passages of Scripture where Jesus is recorded as saying He has experienced someone with great faith.

Now when Jesus had entered Capernaum, a centurion came to Him, pleading with Him, saying, "Lord, my servant is lying at home paralyzed, dreadfully tormented." And Jesus said to him, "I will come and heal him." The centurion answered and said, "Lord, I am not worthy that You should come under my roof. But only speak a word, and my servant will be healed. For I also am a man under authority, having soldiers under me. And I say to this one, 'Go,' and he goes; and to another, 'Come,' and he comes; and to my servant, 'Do this,' and he does it." When Jesus heard it, He marveled, and said to those who followed, "Assuredly, I say to you, I have not found such great faith, not even in Israel! And I say to you that many will come from east and west, and sit down with Abraham, Isaac, and Jacob in the kingdom of heaven. But the sons of the kingdom will be cast out into outer darkness. There will be weeping and gnashing of teeth" (Matthew 8:5-12).

Now read Matthew chapter 15:

Then Jesus went out from there and departed to the region of Tyre and Sidon. And behold, a woman of Canaan came from that region and cried out to Him, saying, "Have mercy on me, O Lord, Son of David! My daughter is severely demon-possessed." But He answered her not a word. And His disciples came and urged Him, saying, "Send her away, for she cries out after us." But He answered and said, "I was not sent except to the lost sheep of the house of Israel." Then she came and worshiped Him, saying, "Lord, help me!" But He answered and said, "It is not good to take the children's bread and throw it to the little dogs." And she said, "Yes, Lord, yet even the little dogs eat the crumbs which fall from their masters' table." Then Jesus answered and said to her, "O woman, great is your faith! Let it be to you as you desire." And her daughter was healed from that very hour (Matthew 15:21-28).

These passages of Scripture are the only two accounts in the Word of God where Jesus is recorded as saying that He saw great faith. In both instances, He said that about an individual who was *not* a covenant person. One was a centurion; he was a Roman and a non-Jew. The other was a Syro-Phoenician woman—a Canaanite and a non-Jew. Now this speaks to the fact that, again, faith is not a Christian matter. Faith is a law in the earth, and will work for anyone who will work it. However, the Christian has access to the God-Kind of Faith. The vital principle of faith is that faith speaks what it believes, and according to James, Bible Faith is "conviction or persuasion plus corresponding action."

Bible Faith is not just believing; it requires putting action to your belief. And the primary action of Bible Faith is that faith speaks what it believes. The mental disposition is that faith speaks what it believes in the present tense, which means faith *is* always *is*. It is always now. Faith is never "will," "God will," or "God is going to." Faith *is* always *is*. God *is*, or whatever the Word says that is.

Here, Jesus articulated that He saw great faith in two people who were not covenant people. I began to look at this, and said, "God, what are the elements here that caused Jesus to say that this is great faith?" Because if it is great faith, and it is in my Bible, then I can have it. I want to know what the elements are that Jesus said make for great faith because I want my faith to work great in every area of my life. I want everything that God says. I want to get it God's way. I want to do it according to the plan and will of God. Understand, first of all, that *you* can have great faith. Great faith is a product of a couple things that the Spirit of the Lord began to reveal to me.

Let's look again at Matthew chapter 8, where this Roman citizen said to Jesus, "Listen, I have a servant who is grievously tormented, and if you will just speak the word only, my servant *will* be healed." The Scripture reads: *"The centurion answered and said, 'Lord, I am not worthy that You should come under my roof. But only speak a word, and my servant will be healed"* (Matthew 8:8). Remember that this was Jesus operating under the Old Covenant, and the centurion was not a covenant child. So when he said, "I am not worthy," he was right. First of all, the centurion was a Roman; he was not a seed of Abraham. In the Old Covenant, the price for redemption had not been paid in full. But for a *blood-bought, Spirit-filled, New Testament child of God to say,* "I am not worthy" is wrong! Why? Because you have been *made* worthy by the blood of Jesus Christ, so don't go to God saying, "I am not worthy" and think that is faith, because you have just contradicted what He has said in His Word about you.

The Bible says that, *"For He made Him who knew no sin to be sin for us, that we might become the righteousness of God in Him"* (2 Corinthians 5:21). I am not unworthy; I am the righteousness of God in Christ Jesus. I am worthy of everything I get! Everything I receive, every blessing I get, I am worthy of; I am worthy not because of who *I am*, but worthy because of *whose I am*. I am connected to the Lord Jesus; I am in Him, and if you are in Him then you cannot be unworthy. My Bible says, "I have been made"; not "I will become." He presents us *"...holy, and blameless, and above reproach in His sight"* (Colossians 1:22). I said, "In *His* sight." It doesn't matter how I look in yours. You did not die for me, and you are not blessing me! It is just a fact—you and I are worthy of the goodness of God through Jesus Christ.

Watch what the centurion said: *"For I am also a man under authority, having soldiers under me. And I say to this one, 'Go,' and he goes; and I say to another one, 'Come,' and he comes; and I say to another one, 'Do this,' and he does it"* (emphasis added).

Now, when Jesus said, *"I have not found such great faith,"* He was not talking, at this point, about the man's faith in Him. He was talking about the man's understanding of the principle that gets things done. The centurion said, "The reason I believe in You is because I know when I say something, with the authority I have, it comes to pass. I understand this is an authority matter. It is based on what you speak. I am a man under authority; and when I say something, I do not go somewhere and say, 'I hope it happens.' Because I have authority, when I tell somebody to go do something, I just go back to the house and expect it to be done. I do not go around worrying, 'I wonder if they are going to do it, I wonder if it is going to happen.' No, I have got the authority to speak!" Basically, he said, "Because I understand how this principle works, I know that You do not have to come to my house."

Great faith is the kind of faith that does not always have to have Jesus physically in the house, as long as you are in the house with His Word! I do not have to have Jesus come and check on me to see if I need anything. He has already come and taken care of everything I need. He is now gone, and He has given me authority to speak His Word! Jesus does

119

not have to come and see about me because the Word is near me in my mouth. I am anointed, authorized, and inspired to handle it; I am learning how this faith principle works.

When Jesus said, "I have not found this kind of faith, not even in Israel," He was saying, "I have not seen this kind of faith in My covenant people. Here is a man who does not even have a covenant with Me, Who understands how this works." Why is it that people without a covenant seem to work this principle better than people with a covenant? I asked God, "Why is it that unbelievers seem to work this principle better than believers?" He said, "Because unbelievers understand that they do not have anybody to depend on

"Great faith speaks and then it believes that what it speaks will happen."

but themselves. So, they know if anything is going to get done, they have to do it. Religion has duped My people into believing that I [Jesus] am going to do everything, when the fact of the matter is, I have already done everything, and now you have to put what I have done to work."

When you get to the point that you stop depending on Jesus to come to your house and look in on you, and understand that you have the authority to deal with circumstances, they will start changing in your life. Great faith *believes* that what it speaks will happen. Great faith *speaks*, and then it *believes* that what it speaks will happen.

Again, you must believe that what you say will come to pass. In Mark 11:23, Jesus said, *"For assuredly, I say to you, whoever says to this mountain, 'Be removed and be cast into the sea,' and does not doubt in his heart, but believes that those things he says will be done, he will have whatever he says."* The key is that you have to say it and believe what you say will be done.

I asked God, "How can I make sure that what I say will be done?" Part of our problem is that we do not believe what we say will be done because we lie to ourselves *all* the time. Often you cannot even trust your own word! Even unintentionally sometimes, you say something you mean to do, and something just keeps it from happening. But it is never so with God's Word. He said, *"Heaven and earth will pass away, but My words will by no means pass away"* (Mark 13:31).

So, how do I make sure that what I am saying, I believe will happen? I stop saying what I am saying and start saying what He has said. If I say what He has said, then I am sure that what He *has said* will come to pass. Now get this: **He did not say that I** *will have what He said* **I'll have. He said I will have** *what I say* **I have.** Just because He said *it*, does not mean I will get *it*. I will not get *it* unless *I* say it. He has said it, but I do not get it unless *I say it.*

Look at Mark 11:23 again: *"For assuredly, I say to you, whoever says to this mountain, 'Be removed and be cast into the sea,' and does not doubt in his heart, but believes that those things he says will be done, he will have whatever he says."* So, even though God has said *it*, if I do not say *it*, I am not getting it. **Great faith believes that what it says will come to pass.** I make sure that I am believing what I say will come to pass by making sure that I am saying what God has said, because He already told me that His Word will not return void (see Isaiah 55:11).

The passage regarding the Syro-Phoenician woman (see Matthew 15:21-28) is vitally important. She was a Gentile, a

Syro-Phoenician woman, who was also outside of the covenant. She said to Jesus, "Listen, my daughter is severely demon-possessed." The Bible says that when she came and said that, Jesus did not say a word to her. Then, she came again, and with persistence she was determined to stay there. Look at Matthew 15:23: *"But He answered her not a word. And His disciples came and urged Him, saying, 'Send her away, for she cries out after us.' But He answered and said, 'I was not sent except to the lost sheep of the house of Israel' "* (emphasis added). Now, do not miss that statement, for within it is the reason why He is not responding to her.

It is not that He did not want to help her, but rather that He had been sent on a mission to the lost sheep of the house of Israel. For this same reason, when He sent out His disciples in Matthew 10:5, He told them to not go into any way of the Gentiles. "Do not go into the city of the Samaritans—only go to the lost sheep of the house of Israel, because that is the area of authority I have been given in My earthly ministry."

He did not respond to her because she was *not* approaching Him on the basis of covenant; she did not have *a covenant*! But Jesus' God is a *covenant* God! If you are trying to get things from God without His covenant, He cannot respond. To put it another way: *"Now this is the confidence that we have in Him, that we if ask anything according to His will, He hears us"* (1 John 5:14). This means if we do not ask according to His will, He does not hear us. And, if I ask anything according to His will, it means I am asking according to the covenant because the covenant is the will. You could start calling the New Testament, the New Agreement, because we do not often use the words *covenant* or *testament* in everyday English.

So, there is an Old Agreement and a New Agreement, and you must deal with God based on your agreement. This woman was Syro-Phoenician, outside of covenant, and did not have an agreement at all. *"Then she came and worshiped Him, saying, 'Lord, help me!' But He answered and said, 'It is not good to take the children's bread and throw it to the little dogs' "* (Matthew 15:25-26). Again, this was a covenant matter. He said, "What you are asking for belongs to the children. Healing belongs to the children." The children of whom? The children of Abraham. He was the one whom the covenant was made with. So, He said, "I cannot, right now, take the bread from the children and give it to the dogs. It is the children's bread." In other words, "The covenant is what gives you a right to the bread." She said in verse 27: " 'Yes, Lord, yet *even the little dogs eat the crumbs which fall from their masters' table.' Then Jesus answered and said to her, 'O woman, great is your faith!' "* (emphasis added).

It has been preached that the reason she received her request is because of her persistence, but *persistence alone* will not get you *anything.* Just because you are persistent does not mean you are going to receive! Again, you have evidence for that—you have been praying, fasting, rolling on the floor, crying, knocking, and seeking. Let me give it to you this way—just because you have a big sledgehammer does not mean you are going to chop down a tree. You are persistent, but you do not have the right instrument. There is no edge on what you are using.

Even if you hit a tree in the same place over and over with a sledgehammer, you will not be yelling "timber" for several years! This is what a lot of Christians do: They hit in the same place, but not with the right instrument—there's no edge on what they are hitting with. It *was not* this woman's persistence that caused her to receive her request. Understand that Jesus denied her on the basis that she was not in the covenant. He said, "Listen, I was sent only to the lost sheep of the house of Israel," which basically says, "This is only for covenant people."

"Great faith sees itself in the covenant."

Secondly, He said, "It is not right for Me to take the children's bread and give it to the dogs. The covenant people, the children, have a right to this, but if you are not in the covenant, you do not have the right." Now remember, Old Covenant was for Israel, but there was a New Covenant coming, which was for everybody.

So this woman said, "Yes, Lord, yet even the little dogs eat the crumbs which fall from their masters' table." What she actually said was, "Yes, I understand that, *but* there has to be a place in this covenant for me. This is *so* good. I see myself in this covenant. Now, I am a little ahead of my time, but I see myself in the **covenant!**" And Jesus says, "O woman, great *is* your faith!" Why? **Because great faith sees itself in the covenant!** Understand what the Bible says in Galatians chapter 3:

> *Christ has redeemed us from the curse of the law, having become a curse for us (for it is written, "Cursed is everyone who hangs on a tree"), that the blessing of Abraham might come upon the Gentiles in Christ Jesus, that we might receive the promise of the Spirit through faith....And if you are Christ's, then you are Abraham's seed, and heirs according to the promise (Galatians 3:13-14,29).*

He is saying that if you are Christ's, then you are Abraham's seed, and you now have a right to everything God promised Abraham. Christ gets you into the covenant by association. You have to be in the covenant; and once you get into the covenant, you have to get into the agreement, which is with Abraham and his Seed. *"Now to Abraham and his Seed were the promises made. He does not say, 'And to seeds,' as of many, but as of one, 'And to your Seed,' who is Christ"* (Galatians 3:16). Get this revelation! It is not to Abraham and his *seeds*; it is to Abraham and his Seed. So when God said to Abraham, "I am making this promise to you and your Seed," He was talking about Abraham and Christ.

God's covenant is not with each one of us. God's covenant is with Abraham, so you have to be of the *Seed* of Abraham, not seeds. He has a covenant with Abraham. The only people who get in on that covenant are people who have the faith of Abraham, not people who are of Abrahamic faith.

Abraham's seed is not Abraham's descendants. Abraham's seed are people who have Abraham's faith or faith like Abraham. What kind of faith did Abraham have? He had the kind of faith that heard God, obeyed God, and said what God said. So, under the Old Covenant, you have to have faith like Abraham. Under the New Covenant, you have to *act* like Jesus.

If you have faith like Abraham, you will benefit under the Old Covenant. If you have faith like Jesus, you benefit under the New Covenant. Though you may be a descendent of Abraham, if you do not act like Abraham, you do not benefit from *that* covenant. Even if you are born again, but you do not *act* like Jesus, you likewise do not get in on *this* covenant.

Therefore, it is not just a matter of getting saved. The question is, since you've been saved, have you started acting like Jesus? Do you speak to situations like He did? Do you command circumstances to come into order by the Word of God, like He did? If you do, then you will benefit from this covenant.

When the woman said in Matthew 15:27, "*Yes, Lord, yet even the little dogs eat the crumbs which fall from their masters' table,*" it meant that even other people can get in on this because it is a covenant matter. She said, "Listen, I see myself partaking of this covenant."

Now, look at Galatians 3:29 again: "*And if you are Christ's, then you are Abraham's seed, and heirs according to the promise.*" This means that if you are Christ's, then every promise that God has made in both covenants belongs to you. But, like this Syro-Phoenician woman, *you have to see yourself in the covenant.* You do that by speaking God's Word concerning you. You have to put yourself in the Word. Great faith is a product of seeing yourself in the promise and speaking yourself into the promise. In other words, I do not say, "Blessed *shall you be* in the city"; I say, "Blessed *am I* in the city." Clarence is blessed in the city, and blessed in the field. Blessed *is* Clarence's basket and his store. Blessed *is* Clarence when he comes in, and when he goes out. Blessed *is* he in the city, and in the fields. Blessed *are* the flocks of his herds and the increase of his cattle. I say, "Clarence's enemies come before him one way, and flee before him seven ways." What am I doing? I am putting myself and seeing myself in the covenant.

Someone may say, "Well, Bishop, the Bible says that we are not supposed to add anything to the Word of God, or take anything away." Listen again. I am not adding anything. I am in there. He said: *"And if you are Christ's, then you are Abraham's seed, and an heir...."* I am not adding anything. When God spoke it, He had me in mind! I am not adding my name to it; I am already in there!

Do you not know that your name is written in the Lamb's Book of Life? Do you think your name is written there so God knows you are supposed to be in Heaven when you get there? No! Your name is written in the Lamb's Book of Life, so when you speak the Word, the angels have record of your authority to operate in Jesus' name, authority, and words! You are not adding anything. You are already registered. Your name is written in the Lamb's Book of Life for right now, not for later. The angels know that this covenant is yours.

It does not matter how big the mountain is; the only thing the angels are looking for is your name! It is a covenant matter! **Great faith believes that what it says will happen because great faith speaks what God says. Great faith sees itself in the covenant and says, "I am in there. Every promise that is made is to me."** Lay your hands on yourself and say, "Every promise in there is for me. I am in every Word that God spoke. I am an heir of His covenant. I am an heir of this covenant. I am an heir of every promise. I am Abraham's Seed because I am Christ's."

Beyond Personal Power

Chapter 8

Receiving the End of Your Faith

Chapter 8

Receiving the End of Your Faith

———————

C hild of God, you have been receiving the Word of God and the revelation of faith as I have taught throughout this book. But hear me now: This is a prophetic word that I must get to you in a very practical sense because it requires some instruction to step into. If you will simply hear, there is nothing else to do except receive. In the name of Jesus, the Lord will grant you what you desire of Him. Take First Peter chapter 1 into your spirit for this prophetic declaration:

In this you greatly rejoice, though now for a little while, if need be, you have been grieved by various trials, that the genuineness of your faith, being much more precious than gold that perishes, though it is tested by fire, may be found to praise, honor, and glory at the revelation of Jesus Christ, whom having not seen you love. Though now you do not see

Receiving the End of Your Faith

Him, yet believing, you rejoice with joy inexpressible and full of glory, receiving the end of your faith—the salvation of your souls (1 Peter 1:6-9).

My presbytery and I were in prayer one day when the Spirit and the anointing of God literally fell, and the presbytery began to share this word. Little did they know that the Spirit of God had put that same word in me several days before—it was a confirmation. The Holy Ghost said to me, "Son, I want you to declare to this people that they are receiving the end of their faith, but also to help them understand what that means and how to do it."

In First Peter 1:9, the Bible says, "*receiving the end of your faith,*" which is "*the salvation of your souls.*" The soul of man is the mind, the will, and the emotions. Now the word *salvation* here is *soteria,* which means the complete deliverance or release. When you came to Christ Jesus and were born again, your spirit became as saved as it will ever be. Your spirit cannot get any more saved; you are redeemed, reconciled, and have been made one in spirit with God. The Bible says that "*He who is joined to the Lord is one spirit with Him*" (1 Corinthians 6:17). The work for the Christian now is discipline, working out; and this is why the Bible says, "*…work out your own salvation in fear and trembling*" (Philippians 2:12). What has to be worked out is your soul's salvation, which basically means getting your mind, will, and emotions to catch up with the truth that is already happening within your spirit.

When Peter says "*the end of your faith,*" he means the objective of your faith. The picture here is of a runner in a race and the end of your faith is the tape at the finish line. Please hear this: The end of your faith is not your manifestation. If you will

131

learn how to receive the end of your faith, your manifestation is only a little while away. If today you can receive the end of your faith, whatever you are believing, desiring, and praying for—whatever God has promised, even though the enemy has impeded and circumstance has said will never happen—is going to fall like a tumbler into your life. **Receiving the end of your faith is the salvation or the deliverance of your mind, will, and emotions**.

Again, let me qualify that Bible Faith is conviction or persuasion plus corresponding action. Faith has both a vital principle and a mental disposition. The vital principle of faith is that faith *speaks* what it believes. The mental disposition of faith is that faith is always *present tense* or *now*! So when the Bible talks about receiving the end of your faith, it is talking about receiving the end of your conviction or persuasion or what you believe plus your corresponding action. This is what speaking what you believe in the present tense, renewing your mind, and making sure the Word of God is constantly coming out of your mouth, is all about. It is about getting you to the place where you can receive the *"end of your faith,"* which is the deliverance of your mind, will and emotions. Now please get this: When Peter says *"the end of your faith,"* the objective is speaking God's Word. And this is why God says, "Speak My Word," in the present tense, like you have it. If you do that, you will receive the end of your faith, and the manifestation will fall just like that.

Remember, the end of your faith is the salvation of your soul. And when Peter says "salvation of your soul," he is not talking about the rapture when the soul is ultimately redeemed. That is the ultimate manifestation of the salvation of your soul. But here he is talking about that dimension that the child of God—the man or woman of faith—gets to where the mind, will, and emotion are no longer susceptible to the vicissitudes of this three-dimensional temporal world. It is the place where no matter what they see or hear or what the devil or their feelings say, their mind is so set and their will is so established that nothing which happens in this three-dimensional world will affect their covenant responsibility or performance. It is a covenant matter!

This is why Heaven will be so heavenly. Heaven is the ultimate redemption not just because it is Heaven. (It is not about geography. I do believe in Heaven. I am going there! But I am not waiting for it—I am not waiting to get there. I have learned that I have the power to bring it to me.) Heaven will be so heavenly because finally your mind, will, and emotions are beyond the grasp of this three-dimensional world. So, finally when you are in Heaven, nothing that happens down here will affect you. This is what the old saints used to say, "No more crying over there and no more dying over there; no more tears over there." Finally, I will be beyond the reach of where temporal changes and shifts affect me. I have got news for you. God expects to have a people on earth so established that their days are as the days of heaven on earth (see Deuteronomy 11:21).

You must get God's Word in your mind, will, and emotions. I have taught that the way to get it in your heart is to get it in your mouth first. That is an order. Remember that Romans 10:8 (KJV) says, *"The word is nigh thee, even in thy mouth, and in thy heart...."* It has to be in your mouth before it gets in your heart. That used to bother me because I thought, "Well, God, it is not right for me to quote Scripture if it is not in my heart." He said, "Son, it is not going to get in your heart until it gets in your mouth. It does not get in your heart by reading it. It gets in your heart by saying it."

Deuteronomy 11:18 reads, *"Therefore you shall lay up these words of Mine in your heart and in your soul, and bind them as a sign on your hand* [if you have to] *and they shall be as frontlets between your eyes."* If your situation is so bad that you cannot remember Scripture and you cannot say anything else, write it on your hand and say, "Wait a minute, devil, let me read this to you: *"And my God shall supply all* [my] *need according to His riches in glory by Christ Jesus"* (Philippians 4:19). Therefore my need is met. I may not be able to quote it, but I can read it. *"He was wounded for our transgressions, He was bruised for our iniquities…"* (Isaiah 53:5). Now we do not wear frontlets, but we do wear baseball caps; put it on your bill if you have to. What is the point? You have to keep this Word in front of your eyes.

> *You shall teach them to your children, speaking of them when you sit in your house, when you walk by the way, when you lie down, and when you rise up. And you shall write them on the doorposts of your house and on your gates* (Deuteronomy 11:19-20).

He said you shall teach them to your children—which is not by taking them to church. You drop your kids off at church, and when they rear up like devils, you complain that the church did not do its job. But it was not the church's fault. You were supposed to be speaking the Word while sitting in your house so they could hear it. Remember verse 19 reads, *"You shall teach them to your children, speaking of them when you sit in your house, when you walk by the way…."* It says speaking—not letting them watch Christian videos. You have to speak God's Word to your children. Now if you do not ever sit in your house, then you cannot speak God's Word in your house, can you? That is one of the problems with our generation. We are always moving everywhere—we have got to do this, that and the other. We do not have any time to sit in the house and speak the Word. Put it on your door so that when you come in after a bad day and the devil has whispered words of defeat, the first thing you see is, *"Blessed shall you be in the city, and blessed shall you be in the country….Blessed shall be your basket and your kneading bowl. Blessed shall you be when you come in, and blessed shall you be when you go out"* (Deuteronomy 28:3,5-6). Whatever you have to do to get the Word in your mouth—by any means necessary—do it.

> *And you shall write them on the doorposts of your house and on your gates, that your days and the days of your children may be multiplied in the land which the Lord swore to your fathers to give them, like the days of the heavens…* (Deuteronomy 11:20-21).

The Father is saying that the whole objective of *"walking by faith and not by sight"* (2 Corinthians 5:7), speaking God's Word in the present tense, and saying you have it even when you do not see it, is to receive the end of your faith. And the end of your faith is getting into that zone where your mind, will and emotions no longer dictate what you believe or do. But if God says it, then it is so.

Receiving the end of your faith—the salvation and deliverance of your soul—is being tapped into that realm, which will be a reality in heaven—where your mind, will and emotions are beyond the grasp of natural, temporal circumstance. God says that that is what happens when you walk by faith, which is why people do not understand you, call you crazy, and say you have lost your mind. They see that there is no car in your garage, but you are saying you have it and they are wondering where it is. What they do not understand is that you are beyond the realm that the fact your garage is empty dictates to you that you do not have it.

Why is this important? Because when people get to the realm where they receive the end of their faith, what they see or do not see does not change their covenant performance. For three years, the church that I oversee has been walking by faith and believing God (for something specific). A lot of people have become impatient because they never believed that it would take this long; and because they did not see anything instantly, they went somewhere where it was easier. These people were moved by what *they did not see*; and because it did not come to pass when they thought it should have, they jumped ship. That will happen sometimes with saints. See, when you receive the end of your faith, what happens or does not happen does not change your covenant performance. Whether it happens in a day or six months you keep on praising, serving, rejoicing, tithing, and giving. When one receives the end of their faith, their soul gets beyond what they see or do not see. So you say, "Well, Bishop, how do I do that?" Here are the instructions.

Remember First Peter 1:6, "*In this you greatly rejoice....*" How do you receive the end of your faith? *Number one: You begin to greatly rejoice.* The Spirit of the Lord said to me, "If you are ever going to receive the end of your faith, command this people to rejoice greatly," which means boisterously, exuberantly, and consistently. Now hear this, child of God—rejoicing is different from praise. Praise is for something: Praise God for His mighty acts and His excellent greatness. Rejoicing can only be done by the spiritually mature because rejoicing is not for anything in the physical temporal realm. To rejoice means to re-fill with joy. *"The joy of the Lord is your strength"* (Nehemiah 8:10). Rejoicing is not just for anything or any-one—the child of God who makes up his mind to rejoice does so because he understands that that is the way he stays strong! It is a decision.

When you get weak, weary, and discouraged, it takes a spiritual person to say, "You know what? I am going to turn off the TV, take the phone off the hook, close the door, and pull down the blinds. I have absolutely no reason to be happy, but I am going to lift up my hands and start jumping and praising God. I rejoice because I have to in order to live." Listen! No matter how bad the news is when you get home, it will not make you stop breathing. I do not care what you are told, it will *not* make you stop breathing. Why? Because you have to breathe to live. So no matter how bad the news is, nothing should be able to keep you from rejoicing because that is what you have to do to live in the Spirit.

The second instruction First Peter gives to receiving the end of your faith is *"the genuineness of your faith must be revealed."* In other words, if you are going to receive the end of your faith, **you have to walk in genuine faith**—not televi-sion faith, not tape series faith—but Bible Faith. God says you have to rejoice and make sure that your faith is genuine, not just believing. It must be actual faith, which means it is not only believing but also being spoken, declared, and acted upon.

Beyond Personal Power

God says if you will do that, you are right now receiving the end of your faith, and once you break the tape at the finish line the manifestation will surely follow without your effort or having to figure it out. This is what the Bible means in First John 5:4 where it says, *"And this is the victory that has overcome the world—our faith."* Faith is not when you get what you are believing for; faith is when you get to the place that nothing in this three-dimensional world changes what you do. God says that that is when you have the victory for real. Once you walk in that dimension—and I am a witness—it is amazing the things that God will pour into your life. Before you have time to pray for things that you didn't even think you needed, He is already sending them your way. You must say, "I am receiving the end of my faith. I am not moved by what I see or do not see. My heart is established. My mind is set. I am trusting in the Lord and walking by faith."

Book of Confessions

Beyond Personal Power

Table of Contents

Table of Contents (continued)

Introduction

Now that you have been instructed in how to experience God's promises by exercising the God-Kind of Faith, it is important for you to declare His Word over your own life and circumstances. God is no respecter of persons. If you and I will put His Word to work, it will produce life in any situation we encounter. That is how powerful God's Word is! In fact, God is so committed to performing His Word that Jesus said it this way: *"Heaven and earth will pass away, but My words will by no means pass away"* (Matthew 24:35).

Remember, faith speaks what it believes in the present tense, and if you believe the Word of God, then your confession should be that God will allow Heaven and earth to crumble before He will allow even one of His promises to fail. As believers, our assurance is that God's promises are for us—for our future, our purpose and our livelihood. However, we must get the Word of God in our mouth and in our heart so that what God has established in Heaven can be manifested here on earth.

Beyond Personal Power

Living faith is a disciplined faith. It is a faith that speaks the Word of God and acts on His promises even when natural circumstances seem to contradict the hope that we have in Him. But, God's Word is true. *"Now this is the confidence that we have in Him, that if we ask anything according to His will, He hears us. And if we know that He hears us, whatever we ask, we know that we have the petitions that we have asked of Him"* (1 John 5:14-15).

God wants the best for His children, but there is a part that you and I have in walking out what is His best for us. *We must speak His Word.* Our attitude must be set in such a way that nothing will discourage us from seeing the fruition of that for which we believe Him to perform. That is the mental disposition, or the vital principle, of faith.

In the following pages, you will see a list of promises from the Bible grouped in categories and written in the present tense, as we are to confess them now. These can be used to begin your confessions of faith. However, I want to encourage you to identify that area in your life where you need God's Word to be manifested—whether it be finances, deliverance, or healing. Whatever it is, find out what God has to say about it, and then you say the same thing. These Scriptures are in no way meant to be exhaustive or to speak on your behalf. That is why it is imperative for you to personalize your confession and search for other Scriptures that speak to your circumstance. Let His Word become alive to you and for you, and watch God begin to work through your confession.

Note: Most Scriptures contained in these confessions have been translated into present tense and personalized format from the New King James Version of the Bible. They have been carefully edited to ensure that none of the original meaning has been corrupted.

Advancing in Ministry

Genesis 30:30

> *For what we had was little and it is now increased to a great amount; for the Lord blessed us.*

Exodus 35:21-22

> *Then everyone comes whose heart is stirred, and everyone whose spirit is willing, and they bring the Lord's offering for the work of the tabernacle of meeting, for all its service, and for the holy garments.*

Exodus 35:29

The children of [name of individual or organization] bring freewill offerings to the Lord, all the men and women whose hearts are willing to bring material for all kinds of work which the Lord, by [leader's name] has commanded to be done.

Exodus 36:1

Every gifted artisan [worker] in whom the Lord has put wisdom and understanding, to know how to do all manner of work for the service of the sanctuary, is doing according to all that the Lord has commanded.

Exodus 36:3b,5b,7

So the people continue bringing to [leader's name], freewill offerings every morning...and the people bring much more than enough for the service of the work which the Lord commanded us to do...and the material that we receive is sufficient for all the work to be done—indeed too much.

Acts 4:32

Now the multitude of those who believe are of one heart and one soul; neither does anyone say that any of the things he possesses are his own, but we have all things in common.

Believing God for a Child

Leviticus 26:9

The Lord looks upon us favorably and makes us fruitful, multiplies us, and confirms His covenant with us.

Deuteronomy 7:14; Exodus 23:26

We are blessed above all peoples; there is not a male or female barren among us.

Beyond Personal Power

Deuteronomy 28:2-4

And all these blessings are come upon us and overtake us because we obey the voice of the Lord our God: we are blessed in the city, and we are blessed in the country. [Wife's name] is blessed in the fruit of her body.

Psalm 128:1-3

We walk in the ways of the Lord…We are happy and it is well with us. We fear the Lord and [wife's name] is a fruitful vine in the heart of our house. Our children are like olive plants, all around our table.

Luke 1:42b

Blessed am I among women, and blessed is the fruit of my womb.

Children

1 Samuel 1:27a-28a

For this child I pray…Therefore I also have lent him (or her) to the Lord; as long as he (or she) lives, he (or she) shall be lent to the Lord.

Proverbs 20:7

I walk in my integrity; my children are blessed after me.

Isaiah 54:13

All our children are taught by the Lord, and great is the peace of our children.

Colossians 3:20

Our children obey us in all things, for this is well pleasing to the Lord.

Confidence/Boldness

Psalm 138:3

In the day when I cried out, You answered me, and made me bold with strength in my soul.

Philippians 4:13

I can do all things through Christ who strengthens me.

Philippians 1:20b

In nothing am I ashamed, but with all boldness, as always, so now also Christ is magnified in my body.

Hebrews 4:16

I therefore come boldly to the throne of grace, that I may obtain mercy and find grace in time of need.

Hebrews 13:6

I say boldly: "The Lord is my Helper; I do not fear. What can man do to me?"

1 John 5:14-15

Now this I have in You, that if I ask anything according to Your will, You hear me. And if I know that You hear me, whatever I ask, I know that I have the petitions I have asked of You.

Deliverance

Psalm 3:3,6

The Lord is a shield for me, my glory and One who lifts up my head. I am not afraid of people who set themselves against me all around.

Psalm 59:1

God delivers me from my enemies and defends me from those who rise up against me.

Psalm 91:3,10,14–16

Surely God delivers me from the snare of the fowler and from the perilous pestilence. No evil befalls me, nor does any plague come near my dwelling; because I set my love upon the Lord, He delivers me; the Lord sets me on high because I know His name. I call upon God and He answers and is with me in trouble; God delivers me and honors me. With long life God satisfies me, and shows me His salvation.

Isaiah 50:2,7-8a

God's hand is not shortened that it cannot redeem…and God has power to deliver. The Lord God helps me; therefore I am not disgraced…and I know that I am not ashamed. He is near who justifies me.

Romans 7:6

I have been delivered from the law, having died to what I was held by, and I serve in the newness of the Spirit and not in the oldness of the letter.

Galatians 3:13

Christ has redeemed me from the curse of the law, having become a curse for me.

Galatians 5:1

I stand fast in the liberty by which Christ has made me free, and I am not entangled again with a yoke of bondage.

2 Timothy 4:18

The Lord delivers me from every evil work and preserves me for His heavenly kingdom.

Titus 2:14

God gave Himself for me, that He might redeem me from every lawless deed and purify me for Himself…and I am zealous for good works.

Beyond Personal Power

Diligence

Proverbs 4:23

I keep my heart with all diligence, for out of it springs the issues of life.

Proverbs 12:27

I am not a lazy person...diligence is my precious possession.

Romans 5:3-4

I glory in tribulation, knowing that tribulation produces perseverance; and perseverance, character; and character, hope.

Romans 12:11

I am not lagging in diligence; I am fervent in spirit, serving the Lord.

2 Timothy 2:15

I am diligent to present myself approved to God, a worker who does not need to be ashamed, rightly dividing the word of truth.

2 Timothy 4:5

I am watchful in all things; I endure afflictions; I do the work and fulfill my ministry.

Hebrews 6:11-12

I show the same diligence to the full assurance of hope until the end, that I do not become sluggish, but imitate those who through faith and patience inherit the promises.

Disciplined Speech, Thoughts, and Actions

Psalm 19:14

> Let the words of my mouth and the meditation of my heart be acceptable in Your sight, O Lord, my strength and my Redeemer.

Psalm 71:8

> My mouth is filled with Your praise and with Your glory all the day.

Psalm 63:3-4

Because Your loving-kindness is better than life, my lips praise You. Thus I bless You while I live; I lift up my hands in Your name.

Philippians 2:11

My tongue confesses that Jesus Christ is Lord, to the glory of God the Father.

Ephesians 4:29-31

No corrupt word proceeds out of my mouth, but what is good for necessary edification, that it may impart grace to the hearers. All bitterness, wrath, anger, clamor, and evil speaking are put away from me, with all malice. I am kind to my brothers and sisters. I am tenderhearted, forgiving, even as God in Christ forgave me.

James 3:13

I am wise and understanding. I show by good conduct that my works are done in the meekness of wisdom.

Faith/Hope

Psalm 71:14

I hope continually and praise You yet more and more.

Acts 27:25

I believe God that it is just as it was told to me.

2 Corinthians 5:7

For I walk by faith, not by sight.

Hebrews 12:1b-2

I lay aside every weight, and the sin which so easily ensnares me, and I run with endurance the race that is set before me, looking unto Jesus, the author and finisher of my faith, who for the joy that was set before Him endured the cross, despising the shame, and has sat down at the right hand of the throne of God.

James 2:18b

I show you my faith by my works [corresponding action].

Hebrews 6:11-12

I show the same diligence to the full assurance of hope until the end. I do not become sluggish, but imitate those who through faith and patience inherit the promise.

Favor

Exodus 3:21

God has given [name of individual or organization] favor in the sight of the people of [person, place, or entity]; and it is so, as we go, that we do not go empty-handed.

Exodus 12:36

And the Lord has given [name of individual or organization] favor in the sight of the people of [person, place, or entity], so that they grant us what we request.

Psalm 102:13,16-17

God is rising and having mercy on [name of individual or organization] for the time to favor her, yes the set time is come. For the Lord is building up [individual or organization]; He is appearing in His glory. He is regarding the prayer of the destitute, and is not despising our prayer.

Psalm 106:4-5

Remember me, O Lord, with the favor You have toward Your people. That I see the benefit of Your chosen ones, that I rejoice in the gladness of Your nation, that I glory with Your inheritance.

Proverbs 3:3-4

Mercy and truth do not forsake me. I bind them around my neck; I write them on the tablet of my heart, and so I find favor and high esteem in the sight of God and man.

Ephesians 3:20

God is able to do exceedingly abundantly above all that I ask or think, according to the power that works in me.

Godly Love

Romans 5:5

Now hope does not disappoint because the love of God has been poured out in my heart by the Holy Spirit who was given to us.

1 Corinthians 13:4-7

I suffer long and am kind; I do not envy; I do not parade myself...I am not puffed up. I do not behave rudely; I do not seek my own; I am not provoked and I think no evil. I do not rejoice in iniquity but rejoice in the truth. I bear all things, I believe all things, I hope all things, I endure all things.

1 John 2:5

I keep God's Word and truly His love is perfected in me. By this I know that I am in Him.

1 John 4:16

I know and believe the love that God has for me. God is love, and I abide in love and in God, and God in me.

1 John 5:3-4

I have the love of God because I keep His commandments. And His commandments are not burdensome. For I am born of God and I overcome the world. And this is the victory that overcomes the world—my faith.

Godly Husband/Wife

Proverbs 12:4a

I am an excellent wife who is the crown of my husband.

Proverbs 31:10-12,25-28

I am a virtuous wife whose worth is far above rubies. The heart of my husband safely trusts me; so he will have no lack of gain. I do him good and not evil all the days of my life. Strength and honor are my clothing; I shall rejoice at all times. I open my mouth with wisdom, and on my tongue is the law of kindness. I watch over the ways of my household, and do not eat the bread of idleness. My children rise up and call me blessed; my husband also, and he praises me.

1 Corinthians 7:3

[Husband's name] renders to [wife's name] the affection due her, and likewise the wife to her husband.

Ephesians 5:22-25

[Wife's name] submits to [husband's name], as to the Lord. For the husband is head of the wife, as also Christ is the head of the church...so let the wives be subject to their own husbands in everything. [Husband's name] loves [wife's name] just as Christ loved the Church and gave Himself for her, that he might sanctify and cleanse her with the washing by the Word.

Godly Staff and Administration

Exodus 35:10

> All who are gifted workers among us are coming and making all that the Lord has commanded.

Exodus 36:1

> Every gifted worker in whom the Lord has put wisdom and understanding knows how to do all manner of work for the service of the sanctuary and is working according to all that the Lord has commanded.

2 Chronicles 29:35b-36

So the service of the house of [name of organization] is being set in order continually. We rejoice that God is preparing us, since the events take place so suddenly.

Isaiah 11:2-3

The Spirit of the Lord rests upon the staff—the spirit of wisdom and understanding, the spirit of counsel and might, the spirit of knowledge and of the fear of the Lord; and we do not judge by the sight of our eyes, nor decide by the hearing of our ears.

Acts 4:32

We who believe are of one heart and one soul; neither does anyone say that any of the things he possesses are his own, but we have all things in common.

Guidance

Psalm 32:8

The Lord instructs me and teaches me in the way I should go; He guides me with His eye.

Psalm 119:105

God's Word is a lamp to my feet and a light to my path.

Proverbs 16:3

My works are committed to the Lord and my thoughts are established.

John 14:26

But the Helper, the Holy Spirit, whom the Father sends in His name, teaches me all things and brings to my remembrance all things that He has said to me.

John 16:13

The Spirit of truth has come, and He guides me into all truth; for He does not speak on His own authority, but whatever He hears He speaks; and He tells me things to come.

Joshua 1:8

This Book of the Law does not depart from my mouth, but I meditate in it day and night, that I may observe to do according to all that is written in it. For then my way is prosperous, and I have good success.

Health/Healing

Exodus 15:26

Because I diligently heed the voice of the Lord my God and do what is right in His sight, I give ear to His commandments and keep all His statutes. He puts no disease on me, for He is the Lord who heals me.

Exodus 23:25

I serve the Lord my God, and He blesses my bread and my water. And He has taken sickness away from the midst of me.

1 Peter 2:24

Christ bore my sins in His own body on the tree, that I, having died to sins, might live for righteousness—by whose stripes I am healed.

3 John 2

I am prospering in all things and I am in good health, just as my soul prospers.

Overcoming Trials and Tribulations

Deuteronomy 33:27

The eternal God is my refuge, and underneath are the everlasting arms; He thrusts out the enemy from before me, and says, "Destroy!"

Isaiah 54:17

No weapon formed against me prospers, and every tongue which rises against me in judgment God condemns.

Romans 8:18,28

The sufferings of this present time are not worthy to be compared with the glory which is revealed in me. And I know that all things work together for good, for I love God and am called according to His purpose.

Romans 8:37

In all things I am more than a conqueror through Christ who loves me.

2 Corinthians 4:17-18

My light affliction, which is but for a moment, is working for me a far more exceeding and eternal weight of glory, while I do not look at the things which are seen, but at the things which are not seen. For the things which are seen are temporary, but the things which are not seen are eternal.

James 1:2-4

I count it all joy when I fall into various trials, knowing that the testing of my faith produces patience. I let patience have its perfect work, that I may be perfect and complete, lacking nothing.

Peace

Isaiah 26:3

God keeps me in perfect peace because my mind is stayed on Him, because I trust in Him.

Psalm 4:8

I lie down in peace, and sleep; for You alone, O Lord, make me dwell in safety.

Psalm 55:18

God has redeemed my soul in peace from battle that was against me.

Psalm 119:165

I have great peace because I love Your law, and nothing causes me to stumble.

Jeremiah 29:11

The Lord knows the thoughts that He thinks toward me, thoughts of peace and not of evil, to give me a future and a hope.

John 14:27

I have the peace that Jesus gives to me. My heart is not troubled, neither do I let it be afraid.

John 16:33

I have peace in Jesus. In the world, there is tribulation; but I am of good cheer because Jesus has overcome the world.

Philippians 4:6-7

I am not anxious for anything, but in everything by prayer and supplication, with thanksgiving, I let my requests be made known to God; and the peace of God, which surpasses all understanding, guards my heart and my mind through Christ Jesus.

Praise and Rejoicing

Exodus 15:2

The Lord is my strength and song, and He has become my salvation; He is my God, and I praise Him. I exalt Him.

Deuteronomy 10:21

God is my praise. He has done for me great and awesome things which my eyes have seen.

Beyond Personal Power

Psalm 5:11

I rejoice in You, Lord; I ever shout for joy, because You defend me; I also love Your name and am joyful in You.

Psalm 9:11

I sing praises to the Lord and declare His deeds among the people.

Psalm 118:24,28

This is the day that You have made. I rejoice and I am glad in it. You are my God and I praise You; You are my God, and I exalt You.

Property/Territory

Exodus 23:20

> *Behold, God has sent an angel before me to keep me in the way and to bring me into the place which He has prepared.*

Deuteronomy 1:8

> *The land is set before me; I go in and possess it.*

Judges 11:24b

> *Whatever the Lord takes possession of before me I do possess.*

Deuteronomy 4:1

I listen to the statutes and judgments which the Lord has taught me to observe; and I live, and go in and possess the land which the Lord is giving me.

Joshua 23:5

The Lord my God expels my adversaries before me and drives them out of my sight, and I possess their land.

2 Samuel 7:10

Moreover the Lord has appointed a place for me and I am planted, and I dwell in a place of my own and move no more; nor do the sons of wickedness oppress me anymore, as previously.

Isaiah 61:7

Instead of my shame, I have double honor, and instead of confusion I now rejoice in my portion. In my land I possess double; and everlasting joy is mine.

Prosperity/Wealth

Deuteronomy 8:18-19

I remember You, O Lord, for it is You who gives me the power to get wealth, that You may establish Your covenant.

Deuteronomy 29:9

I keep the words of the Lord's covenant, and I do them, and I prosper in all that I do.

Joshua 1:7-8

I am strong and very courageous, and I am observing and doing according to the Word of the Lord. I am not turning from it, to the right hand nor the left, and I am prospering wherever I go. The Word of God is constantly in my mouth and I meditate in it day and night. I observe and do according to all that is written in it. I am making my way prosperous and I am having good success.

1 Samuel 30:19

Nothing of mine is lacking, either small or great; and anything which has been taken from me, I have recovered all.

Psalm 35:27

I am shouting for joy and I am glad, and I say continually, "The Lord is magnified and He has pleasure in my prosperity."

Matthew 18:27

Those whom I owe have been moved with compassion, have released me, and forgiven me of debt.

1 Corinthians 2:12

Now I have received, not the spirit of the world, but the Spirit who is from God, and I know the things that have been freely given to me by God.

2 Corinthians 9:8

You make all grace abound toward me, that I, always having all sufficiency in all things, may have an abundance for every good work.

Philippians 4:19

God is supplying all my need according to His riches in glory by Christ Jesus.

Beyond Personal Power

Righteousness

―――✦―――

Deuteronomy 6:18a

I do what is right and good in the sight of the Lord and it is well with me.

Job 27:5b-6

Till I die I do not put away my integrity from me. My righteousness I hold fast and do not let it go; my heart does not reproach me as long as I live.

Isaiah 54:14

In righteousness I am established; I am far from oppression, for I do not fear; and from terror, for it does not come near me.

Psalm 5:7-8

I come into Your house in the multitude of Your mercy; in fear of You I worship toward Your temple. Lead me, O Lord, in Your righteousness because of my enemies; make Your way straight before my face.

Psalm 24:5

I receive blessing from the Lord, and righteousness from the God of my salvation.

Ephesians 4:22-24

I have put off, concerning my former conduct, the old man which grows corrupt, and I am renewed in the spirit of my mind. I have put on the new man which was created according to God, in true righteousness and holiness.

Salvation

Psalm 85:9

Surely salvation is near to me because I fear the Lord, and glory dwells in my land.

Romans 13:11

I know the time, for now my salvation is nearer than when I first believed.

2 Corinthians 6:2

Behold, now is the accepted time; behold, now is the day of salvation.

2 Thessalonians 2:13

God from the beginning chose me [or insert name] for salvation through sanctification by the Spirit and belief in the truth.

Titus 2:11-12

For the grace of God that brings salvation has appeared to me [or insert name], teaching me [or insert name] that, denying ungodliness and worldly lusts, I [she or he] live soberly, righteously, and godly in the present age.

2 Peter 3:9

The Lord is not slack concerning His promise but is longsuffering toward us, not willing that I [or insert name] should perish but that I [or insert name] should come to repentance.

Sanctification

Psalm 86:2,5

God preserves my life, for I am holy. For You, Lord, are good, and ready to forgive, and abundant in mercy to me as I call upon You.

Romans 12:1

I present my body a living sacrifice, holy, acceptable to God, which is my reasonable service.

1 Corinthians 3:16

I am the temple of God and the Spirit of God dwells in me.

1 Corinthians 6:17,20

I am joined to the Lord and am one spirit with Him. I have been bought with a price; therefore I glorify God in my body and in my spirit, which are God's.

Ephesians 1:3-4

God has blessed me with every spiritual blessing in Christ, just as He chose me in Him before the foundation of the world, and I am holy and without blame before Him in love.

Colossians 3:10

I put on the new man who is renewed in knowledge according to the image of God who created me.

Colossians 3:12a

I am the elect of God, holy and beloved.

1 Thessalonians 4:3-4,7

This is the will of God, my sanctification: that I know how to abstain from sexual immorality; that I know how to possess my own vessel in sanctification and honor. For God calls me to holiness.

1 Peter 2:9,11

I am a chosen generation, a royal priesthood, a holy nation, God's own special child, and I proclaim the praises of Him who called me out of darkness into His marvelous light. I abstain from fleshly lusts which war against the soul.

Beyond Personal Power

Strength

Deuteronomy 31:6

I am strong and of good courage, I do not fear and I am not afraid of them; for the Lord my God, He is the One who goes with me. He will not leave me or forsake me.

2 Samuel 22:33

God is my strength and my power, and He makes my way perfect. He makes my feet like the feet of deer, and sets me on my high places.

Psalm 27:1,3

The Lord is my light and my salvation; whom shall I fear? The Lord is the strength of my life; of whom shall I be afraid? Though an army may encamp against me, my heart shall not fear; the war may rise against me, in this I will be confident.

Psalm 46:1

God is my refuge and strength, a very present help in trouble.

Isaiah 41:10

I fear not, for God is with me. I am not dismayed. He strengthens me and helps me; He upholds me with His righteous right hand.

2 Corinthians 12:10

I take pleasure in infirmities, in reproaches, in needs, in persecutions, in distresses, for Christ's sake. For when I am weak, then I am strong.

Ephesians 6:10

I am strong in the Lord and in the power of His might.

Wisdom/Discernment

Job 36:3-4

> *I fetch my knowledge from afar; I ascribe righteousness to my maker. For truly my words are not false; One who is perfect in knowledge is with me.*

Psalm 1:1-2

> *I am blessed because I do not walk in the counsel of the ungodly, nor stand in the path of sinners, nor sit in the seat of the scornful; but my delight is in the law of the Lord and in His law I meditate day and night.*

Proverbs 2:10-12a

Wisdom enters my heart and knowledge is pleasant to my soul. Discretion preserves me; understanding keeps me, to deliver me from the way of evil.

Proverbs 4:7

Wisdom is the principle thing; therefore I get wisdom. And in all my getting, I get understanding.

Daniel 1:17

God has given me knowledge and skill in all literature and wisdom; and I have understanding in all visions and dreams.

Malachi 3:18

I discern between righteous and the wicked, between one who serves God and one who does not serve Him.

1 Corinthians 2:12

Now I have received, not the spirit of the world, but the Spirit who is from God, that I might know the things that have been freely given to me by God.

Beyond Personal Power

Other Materials Available by Clarence E. McClendon Ministries

---

Books

X Blessing

And When You Pray

Audio Tape Series

Reversing a Cursing

Seeds to Your Success

Coming Into a Wealthy Place

The Power to Get Wealth

Clarence E. McClendon Ministries
P.O. Box 78398
Los Angeles, CA 90016

For more information, please visit www.cemm.info

Prayer Request

If you have a prayer request that you would like our ministry to pray over, please write the following information on a separate sheet of paper and mail it to the address below. Thank you.

Print Name

Address

City, State, and Zip Code

Phone Number

Email Address

Prayer Request

Please mail your prayer request to:

C.O.T.H.I.
P.O. Box 78398
Los Angeles, CA 90016